LEARN TO WEAVE

with ANNE FIELD

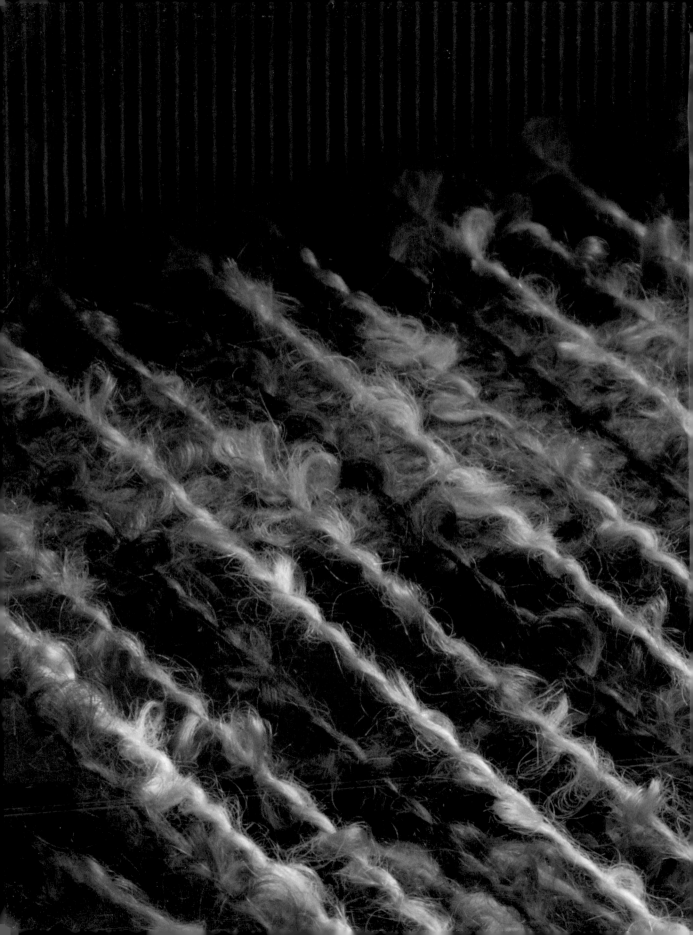

Acknowledgements

This is the hardest part of writing the whole book. How do you thank all those who made it possible?

To my son-in-law Tony, who not only took most of the photos but who has helped me out of numerous computer mishaps (and never laughed at me once), I owe a big thanks. I am so lucky he married my daughter Jane. She now weaves full time, and has helped me by answering many questions and weaving the floor rug in Chapter 12.

To Mike Wakelin for the drawings, John Hunter for the modelled photos, and a big thanks to Schacht Looms, to Jane and Barry. I began this book when the big earthquake of February 2011 struck Christchurch, and during the process of setting up a new studio, they supplied the Baby Wolf loom and all the extra equipment I needed for this book.

To my editor and all those at Bateman who surpass my expectations of what this book will look like — I am very appreciative of all the work that goes into a manuscript before it finally reaches you, the readers.

And lastly, to those weavers over the years who have passed on their skills, I hope I do you credit!

Anne Field
February 2013

Foreword

Anne Field died on the 29th May 2013.

Anne (my mother) had finished writing this book and was starting to do the final checks before it was to go to her publisher. Her drive and determination to finish it, even though she was very ill, is a reflection of her passion for weaving. Anne got an immense amount of satisfaction from writing about weaving and spinning, and from sharing her knowledge.

Anne taught extensively around the world. The experiences that she shared with her students have helped her write the many books she has published over the years. This is her tenth book.

Ironically, this book illustrates how I learnt to weave — through doing projects under instruction when I was growing up. All the small tips that my mother gave me along the way are written here. It has been a privilege to help in the final stages of completion of this book, her last work.

Jane Clark
January 2014

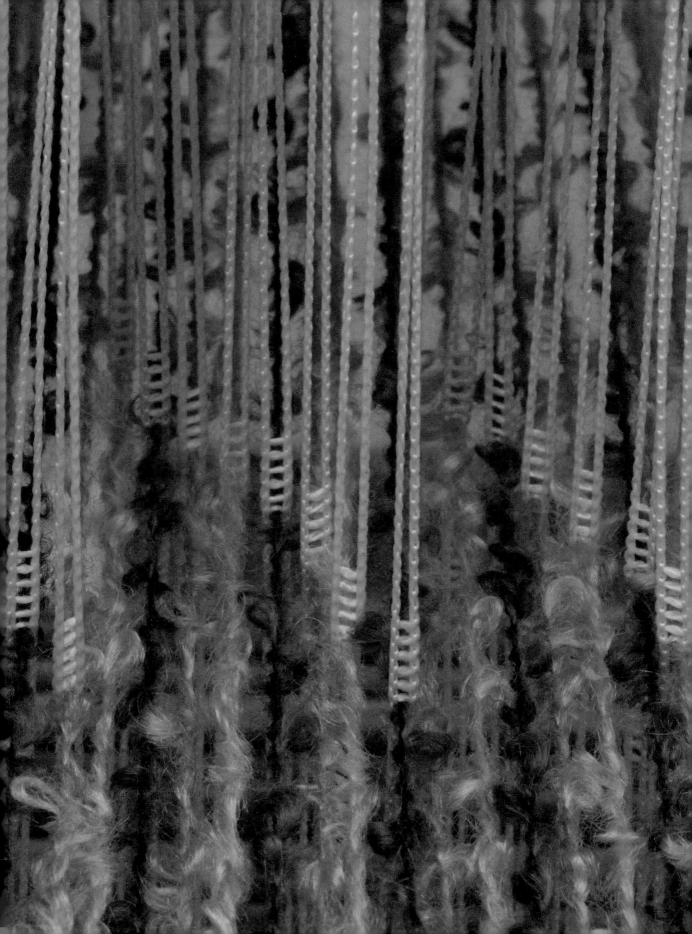

Contents

Contents

Introduction

WEAVERS and spinners are a very caring group. We share our sources, yarns, books and equipment with anyone who asks. This book is an accumulation of over 50 years of weaving. Over those 50 years, hundreds of weavers have shared their knowledge, inspiration, enthusiasm and skills with me, and to pass this on is a privilege.

I began weaving with a small 61-cm (24-inch) loom and a book by Elsie Davenport called *Your Hand Weaving*, published in 1948. There were no photos, and the book was crammed with drawings and words I didn't understand, but it started me off on this long journey. Books have changed so much in both the writing and the publishing since that early weaving book. They are now inspirational, colourful and written with the love of our craft shining through. And not only do we have books as one resource, we now have all the internet has to offer: we can Facebook, tweet, google, and join myriads of online groups.

The way I write books has gradually changed. In the beginning, I would describe the basics of threading the loom, then explain different techniques. Each book was loom-based. The first book was for rigid heddle looms, the next for four-shaft table looms and so on. Slowly I added in projects to these books. I would describe the structure of a certain technique and then give a project using this technique. This book begins the other way around. It starts with a project and then gives detailed instructions on how to weave it. It also consists entirely of projects, beginning with a simple scarf and finishing with a fine wool fabric that can be cut into to make a garment.

There are many different approaches to weaving. Some of my students like to have all the planning done for them. They need to know how much yarn to buy and where it comes from.

A second group of weavers will begin with the whole project set out for them. After weaving two or three projects, they begin to change the instructions, use different yarns and colours. They will make mistakes, but this is part of the learning process.

The third group begins with an idea in their heads and no instructions, and will work out the project for themselves. Their projects will be original and unusual. I can remember a young, confident weaver (she had woven one scarf!) who decided to make a hammock. The colours were magical and it looked great in an exhibition. But when it was used a few times, it literally fell to bits as the warp was too weak. We could all see the potential for this weaver; she just needed to learn a few techniques. She needed encouragement without losing the enthusiasm. Sometimes we are discouraging to these adventurous weavers, but they are the ones who will push the boundaries of our craft.

I would like to think that this book can be used by all three types of weavers. Each project is very detailed and can be woven by just following the instructions. But each project can also be changed to reflect the weaver's own taste and knowledge, and each project may stimulate an idea or two, which will lead the weaver in a new direction.

However this book is used, my 50 years of weaving is there for all to share. Sometimes at conferences I meet someone who is wearing something based on one of my projects or ideas. I don't know what my face shows, but inside I am so pleased. To think that my words have taken this weaver to a place where we connect gives me a real thrill. Words are not just communication but are the means of unlocking our creativity. And you will pass on this knowledge to other weavers in turn.

ANNE FIELD

Part I
LEARNING TO WEAVE

What is a loom?

WHEN I BOUGHT my first 'proper' loom, it was a four-shaft table loom. Not that I knew its name at the time. I looked through the small book that I bought with it until I came to a drawing that looked something like my loom. The loom was partly disassembled, so that was my first difficulty. The book said that the length of the reed (the metal comb-like piece sitting in the beater that separates and beats the lengthwise threads) gives you the weaving width. I measured my reed, when I worked out which part it was, and it was 30 inches long. (This was in pre-metric days.) So for three years I thought I had a loom with a 30-inch weaving width. I did have lots of problems when I tried to weave articles 30 inches or more wide, as the threads kept tangling around the ratchets. Eventually, when we moved to a much larger town and I met and talked to real weavers, I found I had a 27-inch loom with a 30-inch reed!

The other problem was caused by these real weavers speaking in a language I didn't understand. 'How many picks to the inch?' 'What did you use for a tabby binder?' 'What is your e.p.i?' Mostly I was too young and stupid to ask for explanations, as I didn't want to appear ignorant. Luckily, my passion for weaving made me persist and very slowly I learnt more about looms and weaving.

ALL LOOMS HAVE SEVERAL ELEMENTS IN COMMON:

1. Frame: This is made commonly of wood, but can also be metal. It must be rigid enough to withstand the tension applied to the **warp**, the lengthwise threads. (Weavers also talk about 'warping', which is the process of arranging the lengthwise threads on the loom in preparation for weaving.)
2. Something to hold, raise and lower the **warp ends**. Here is another tricky use of weaving language. A warp thread is called an 'end'. This lifting device can simply be your fingers, as in a simple frame loom, or it can be a very elaborate mechanism.
3. Most looms, apart from frame looms, have some way of extending the warp length; usually rollers at the front and the back of the loom. Some sort of mechanism is needed to brake and control the rollers. This is often a ratchet and pawl system or a friction brake.

Frame, rigid heddle and inkle looms

- A frame loom is commonly used for tapestry weaving. It is a strong wooden frame on which the warp is wound and the warp ends are raised by lifting every alternate end with your fingers or by attaching string **heddles** (loops) to every alternate end.

1.1 Reed

Warp: Lengthwise threads on a loom

Warp ends: Warp threads

Heddles: Metal or string loops holding warp threads

Weft: Widthwise threads

Shuttle: The yarn holder

Pick: A single weft row

- A rigid heddle loom also has a frame and a beater, which pushes the **weft** (the widthwise threads) down when weaving. The beater contains the holes and slots to hold the warp ends and raise or lower them. These looms usually have some method of extending the warp, such as a ratchet and pawl system.
- Inkle looms are narrow looms, usually with string heddles, as on a frame loom, and some sort of warp lengthening system, such as a selection of pegs you can choose to wind the warp around. They are used mainly for making narrow bands.

▌LOOM TYPES

In this book, I will concentrate on table and floor looms. If you are in the happy position of being able to choose your own loom, go to page 27 and see what each loom type is suitable for. For example, if you want to weave floor rugs, counterbalance or countermarch looms are best. Then read up on those types of looms.

If you have been given a loom, or bought one, as I did, without any knowledge of what type it was, read through the following sections to see what sort of loom you have. Then go to page 28 to see what that loom will weave best.

TABLE LOOMS

See figure 1.A. These stand on a table, and the shafts are raised and lowered by a series of handles. A shaft (sometimes called a 'harness') is a light frame which holds the heddles (short lengths of metal or string with eyes in the centre), through which the warp ends pass.

Advantages
- Portable. Easy to take to workshops.
- Usually smaller in size than floor looms. They can vary from 15cm (6in) wide to 81cm (32in) wide.
- Many table looms can be partially dismantled, even with a warp on, for storage or when carrying them to classes.
- Less expensive.
- Any combination of the 14 shaft possibilities can be used in one piece of weaving, as there is no tying of shafts to treadles.

Disadvantages
- Usually have a limited warp length, depending on the placement of the warp and cloth beams. The warp beam holds the warp at the back of the loom and the cloth beam holds the finished cloth at the front of the loom. The amount of space around these beams determines the length they will hold.
- Because of the positioning of the handles that raise and lower the shafts, you usually have to stand to use this type of loom. This can be tiring.
- To work the handles, the **shuttle**, which carries the weft yarn (page 79), has to be put down between rows (or **picks**, as rows are called in weaving language). This can disrupt the weaving rhythm.

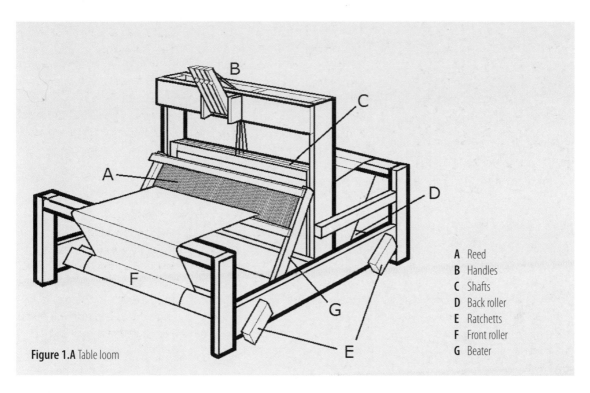

Figure 1.A Table loom

A Reed
B Handles
C Shafts
D Back roller
E Ratchetts
F Front roller
G Beater

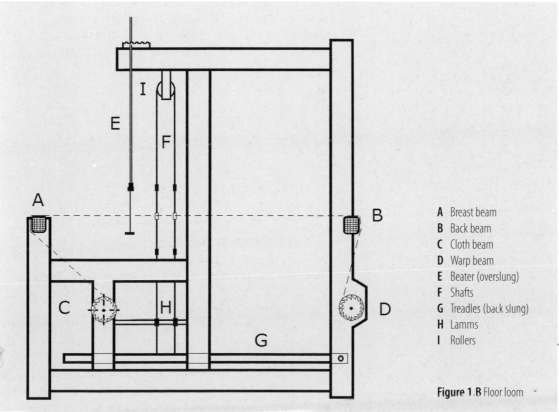

A Breast beam
B Back beam
C Cloth beam
D Warp beam
E Beater (overslung)
F Shafts
G Treadles (back slung)
H Lamms
I Rollers

Figure 1.B Floor loom

- Need a sturdy table to put the loom on. Not knowing this, I had my first table loom on a collapsible card table. As you'd expect, the table used to collapse now and then, so this wasn't a good idea.

FLOOR LOOMS

See figure 1.B, page 19. These stand on the floor and the shafts are raised and lowered by your feet depressing the treadles.

Advantages

- Can be any width, so wider widths of cloth can be woven.
- Less tiring, as you sit down to weave and raise the shafts with foot treadles.
- As the shafts are raised by your feet, your hands are free, so you don't need to put the shuttle down between picks and it is easier to maintain a good rhythm.
- The size and weight of the loom make it very stable.
- Can usually take a longer warp than a table loom.

Disadvantages

- Less portable than a table loom, although some of the smaller floor looms have wheels and can be folded and moved (photo 2.11, page 43).
- Usually more expensive.
- Take up more room.
- The shaft combinations used when weaving are limited by the number of treadles. To change the shaft combinations, the treadles will need to be re-tied to other shafts.

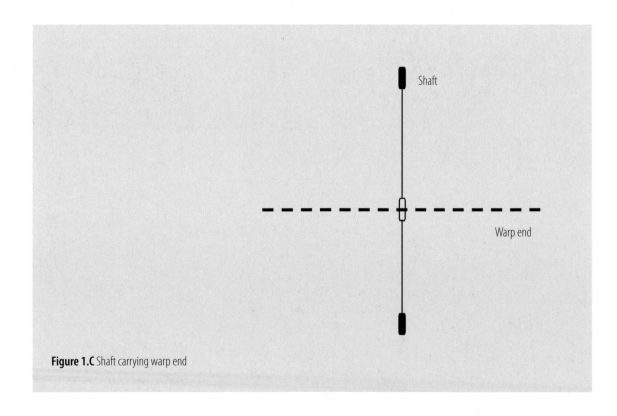

Figure 1.C Shaft carrying warp end

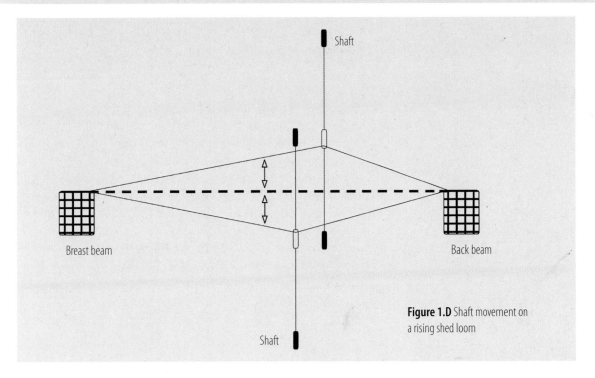

Shaft

Breast beam

Back beam

Shaft

Figure 1.D Shaft movement on a rising shed loom

■ MAIN LOOM TYPES — HOW THEY WORK

Within the categories of floor and table looms are many, many variations, and it is impossible to discuss them all here. Instead I'll focus on a general description of how the main loom types work covering rising shed, counterbalance, countermarch and jack looms.

As mentioned before, all table and floor looms have a way to raise and lower the warp ends to make a **shed**: another odd weaving term which means the gap when some of the shafts are lowered and some are raised. This is where the shuttle passes through. The loom is usually named by the type of mechanism that raises and lowers the shafts.

Each shaft, and there can be as few as two and as many as 44, carries a number of warp ends. There must be at least two shafts to make a shed — one lifting and the second one sinking to make the gap. There are various ways to do this. (Figures 1.C and 1.D)

RISING SHED LOOM

All table looms that I have seen are rising shed looms, where one set of threads on one shaft remain stationary and the other shaft rises when weaving. Jack looms, which are floor looms, also use this system. Because one layer of threads remains stationary, the treadle is depressed the same distance as the height of the shed.

For a rising shed loom to function properly, the lower warp ends should be dropped at the same angle as the other ends will rise. Holding down these lower ends is done in various ways. Sometimes springs hold them down or the weight of the heddles can also do this if they are metal.

> Shed: The gap in the warp through which the shuttle passes

21

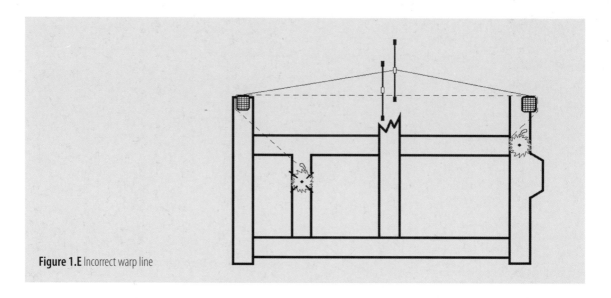

Figure 1.E Incorrect warp line

To check the shaft level, tie two threads onto the breast beam, thread them through two adjacent heddles on two separate shafts and then tie them onto the back beam. At rest, with all the shafts down, the threads should angle down slightly. When you lift one shaft the angle of the upper shed should be equal to the lower shed angle. Because one layer of warp will rise while the other is stationary, rising shed looms are not suitable for weaving floor rugs, which require a very tight tension. When tension is set this tight on a rising shed loom, the lower layer is pulled up, and this can result in a different tension on the upper and lower layers, making firm **beating** difficult.

In figure 1.E you can see what happens if the lower warp end comes in a straight line from the back of the loom to the front. When weaving, the upper layer of warp ends is stretched tight and the lower layer is looser. This uneven tension makes weaving difficult.

The other point with rising shed looms is that the warp ends should rest on the bottom of the reed when all the shafts are down. If they don't lie at the bottom of the reed, two things can happen.

- The shuttle will not easily skim across the lower warp ends while you are weaving. Using a stick shuttle (photo 3.1, page 71) which is placed, not thrown, through the shed is helpful.
- The shed will not be as wide as it should be for the shuttle to pass through smoothly. Using a smaller shuttle will help.

COUNTERBALANCE LOOMS

These are looms where, as one shaft rises, the opposing shaft sinks. This means both upper and lower layers are under the same tension at all times. (Figure 1.F)

Many floor looms are of this type and it is the simplest mechanism for raising and lowering the shafts. This loom has changed little over the centuries and, as the movements are direct and obvious to the

> Beating is the action of pulling the beater towards you to position the last weft pick.

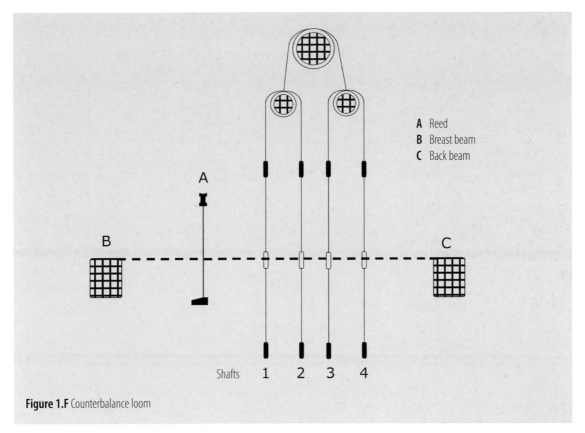

A Reed
B Breast beam
C Back beam

Shafts 1 2 3 4

Figure 1.F Counterbalance loom

weaver, they are easy to understand. The treadling is quiet, smooth and light. These looms usually work on a pulley system, where the rising shaft pulls the opposing shaft down at the same time. This is the same action as a cable car, where the descending car pulls up the ascending car. This makes these looms easy to treadle as there is little weight. (Figure 1.G)

Some looms use 'horses' instead of pulleys to raise and lower the shafts. Horses are short, curved bars of wood with notches at both ends. The ties attached to the shafts fit into the notches and as one end is pulled down by the treadle action, the other end rises. Rollers can also be used.

With counterbalance looms:

- The stationary shed should lie halfway up the reed. This allows for the rising and sinking movement of the shafts.
- Because each shaft is paired with another, for one to go up as the other goes down, it is difficult to lift one shaft on its own. Some four-shaft patterns require 1 shaft up, and 3 down. By using two feet and getting a half shed it can be done (figure 1.Ha, page 24), but the usual practice is to have 2 up and 2 down (figure 1.Hb, page 24). Some counterbalance looms have been fitted with a shed regulator which overcomes this problem.

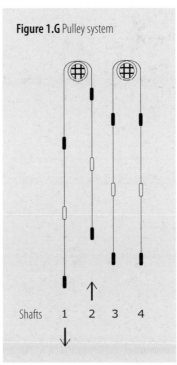

Figure 1.G Pulley system

Shafts 1 2 3 4

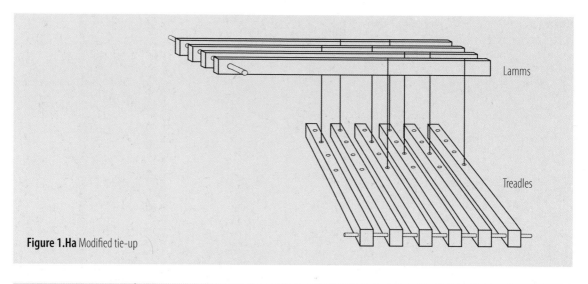

Figure 1.Ha Modified tie-up

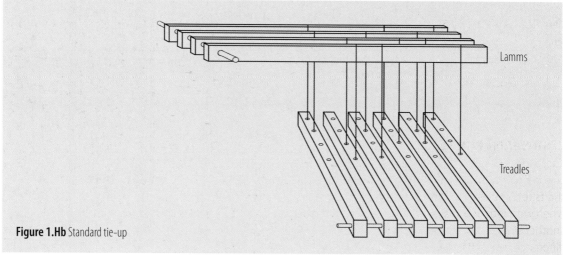

Figure 1.Hb Standard tie-up

- These looms are usually four-shaft. There may be some counterbalance looms with more shafts somewhere, but I have yet to see one.
- These looms have lamms, long wooden levers, pivoted at one side, which lie parallel to the shafts and connect the treadles to the shafts. They allow a direct pull downwards from the shafts when the treadle is pushed down. (Figure 1.B, page 19.)
- Beaters on counterbalance looms can be underslung, pivoted from the lower frame of the loom, or overslung, suspended from the top of the loom. (Figure 1.B shows an overslung beater.)
- You can regulate the size of the shed by pushing harder or softer on the treadles.
- Because one shaft goes up while the other goes down, the treadles need only travel half the distance required on a rising shed loom.

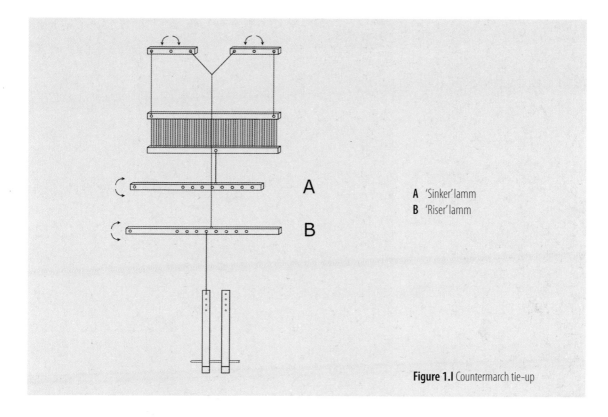

A 'Sinker' lamm
B 'Riser' lamm

Figure 1.I Countermarch tie-up

COUNTERMARCH LOOMS

These looms can be spelled 'countermarche' or as two separate words, counter march, just to confuse us. They have a more complex tie-up of shafts to treadles than the counterbalance loom but give more scope when weaving. Again, as with counterbalance looms, as one shaft rises another sinks, giving equal tension to the ends on both shafts. But the difference here is that each shaft moves independently of the others, allowing any combination of shafts to be raised and lowered. This makes it a very versatile loom. (Figure 1.I)

The lamms are usually of different lengths. The shorter lamm is attached to the bottom of the shaft, causing that shaft to sink when the treadle is depressed, and the longer lamm connects to the **jack** at the top of the loom, causing that shaft to rise when the treadle is depressed.

The countermarch tie-up in figure 1.I has the shaft tied to the riser lamm so when the left treadle is depressed, the shaft will rise. A tie-up is the connection between the shafts and the treadles (figure 3.CF and pages 80–82).

Not only do the different lengths make it easier to distinguish between the lamms that cause the shafts to rise or sink, but as they are connected to different parts of the loom, the weight on each lamm is equalised. When I first got my countermarch loom, I wrote U for up on all the rising lamms and D for down on the sinking lamms. This made it easier to distinguish the difference when I sat under the loom changing the tie-ups.

A **jack** is a pivoted wooden or metal bar.

25

With countermarch looms:

- The stationary warp should lie halfway up the reed to allow for the rising and sinking movement of the shafts.
- There can be any number of shafts on the loom.
- A less common type of countermarch loom has vertical jacks, rather than the more common horizontal ones in figure 1.I, page 25.
- The tie-up of the treadles to the lamms is such that each shaft has two lamms; a rising and a sinking one. For example, on a 4-shaft loom, if you want shaft 1 to rise and the other 3 to sink, you attach shaft 1 to the rising lamm, and shafts 2, 3, 4 to the sinking lamms. Therefore you can't have any shaft tied to both a rising and sinking lamm at the same time. You can see why I labelled my lamms U and D. Figure 1.I shows one shaft tied to the rising lamm.
- You can have an underslung or overslung beater.
- Tying up a countermarch loom is more complex than with a counterbalanced loom, but the extra versatility makes this worthwhile.
- It is important to get the levels of the shafts, lamms and treadles correct so the warp is lying in the middle of the reed when there is no shed. To stabilise the loom before starting this process, put rods through the jacks. To attach all the cords from the jacks to the shafts, lamms and treadles, a warp needs to be on the loom. This can just be a sample of a few ends on each shaft. Each loom should come with instructions on how to do this. If there are no instructions, a good source is Joanne Hall's book, *Tying up the Countermarch Loom*.
- The heddles can be string (photo 1.2, page 31), as the action does not need any weight in the shafts to return them to their resting position.
- Because one shaft goes up while the other goes down, the treadles need only travel half the distance required on a rising shed loom.

JACK LOOMS

These looms are rising shed looms, usually found in the USA. They do not need an overhead support as the shafts are generally pushed up from below. Each shaft acts independently. (Figure 1.J)

- As they have no overhead support, the beater is usually underslung.
- Many of these looms can be folded up, both with or without a warp on, making the smaller types portable. Some will have wheels so they can be folded and transported easily.
- Because there is no overhead **castle**, they appear to take up less space, although the footprint is the same as other floor looms.
- They are noisier, as it is the weight of the shafts which return them to their resting position. To help with this return, the heddles are usually metal (photo 2.11 page 43).
- The warp rests on the bottom of the beater and, as with all rising

> The **castle** is the upper loom frame which suspends the shafts.

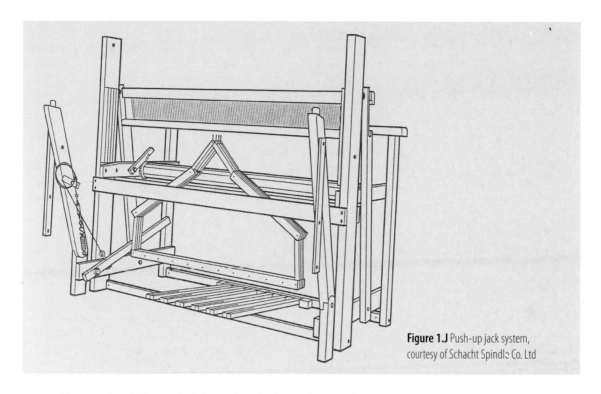

Figure 1.J Push-up jack system, courtesy of Schacht Spindle Co. Ltd

shed looms, should be angled down slightly. Again the metal heddles help keep the warp down in the correct position, as do the rests the shafts are seated on.

• Because one layer of threads remains stationary, the treadle is depressed the same distance as the height of the shed (figure 1.D, page 21), unlike counterbalance and countermarch looms which have a smaller shed.

WHICH LOOM IS BEST FOR YOU?

As a beginner you will probably not know what sort of weaving you will like best. Most experienced weavers end up specialising; for example, they become tapestry weavers, linen weavers, floor rug weavers or perhaps fabric for clothing becomes their favourite type of weaving. However, you are at the beginning of your journey. I began with a smallish table loom, then progressed to a countermarch floor loom, then a computer-assisted dobby loom. Mind you, that covered 50 years or so of weaving! So don't look upon your first purchase as necessarily your last.

There is a ready market for all types of second-hand looms and some of the magazines listed in the bibliography (page 186) will provide valuable information. Attending a class where you try various loom types before buying is an excellent idea, and weaving guilds are another source of information. Some manufacturers can supply names of weavers living near you who are willing to show their looms to prospective buyers. Trade shows are very useful too.

Buying a loom

NEW?

With a new loom, you will get a manual that tells you how the loom works. If it arrives in pieces or has been only partially assembled, I suggest you put it together yourself. This will greatly help with understanding how it works.

OR SECOND-HAND?

It is a big help to have the loom manual. The loom owner may not have the original handbook, but do ask just in case. If you know the maker of your second-hand loom, google the name, as often you can contact them for instructions.

I would never buy a second-hand loom if it wasn't assembled. I need to see it working if possible. As a beginner, you will not know if all the bits are there and it may be impossible or very expensive to get missing pieces made.

Try to get an experienced weaver to come with you to check it out. I can remember going with a student to look at a loom they wanted to buy, only to find it was being used as a pot plant stand. Even then we could see some of the treadles were missing.

Test it for stability. Are any pieces warped? If it has a ratchet and pawl system, are all the teeth present? Metal teeth are much stronger than wooden ones, which can chip and break. If the reed is rusty, this can be fixed (page 30), or replaced, but this is an extra cost. If the heddles are rusty metal ones they can be replaced too.

HOW MUCH TO PAY

If it is a known brand and you have internet access, check the manufacturer's website for the cost of a new loom or visit shops that sell new looms. This will give you an idea of the loom's value. You can also look at the advertisements at the back of hand-weaving magazines, as they usually advertise second-hand looms.

The following comments are general: many loom manufacturers are ingenious and have devised ways to make their looms suitable for a wide range of weaving.

RISING SHED LOOMS

- Best for more lightweight cloth. It is difficult to get a correctly tensioned warp when weaving with strong and inelastic warp threads such as thicker linen for floor rugs or finer linen for table coverings.
- Usually lighter in construction than other looms, so heavy beating for floor rugs is difficult.

COUNTERBALANCE LOOMS

- Ideal for heavy articles such as floor rugs, as they are usually very solid and stable. The split shed gives an ideal tension.
- Not suitable for more complex weaving structures that need one shaft up and the other three down.
- As these require very little pressure on the treadles, they are great if you cannot push down hard on the treadles.
- Usually limited to four shafts.

COUNTERMARCH LOOMS

- The most versatile of looms, suitable for the heavy beating needed for floor rugs and the light beating for delicate cloth.

- As they are more complex to make, they may be more expensive than counterbalance looms.
- You will spend a little more time underneath this type of loom, as each treadle has to be tied to all the shafts. As I get older I find it gets harder to get up from underneath a loom. I can get down fine!

There are other considerations when buying a loom.

UNDERSLUNG OR OVERSLUNG BEATER

Most rising shed looms have no overhead support, so the beater must be pivoted from the lower section of the loom. Most table looms are like this, but there are some that have castles that can support an overslung beater.

Weavers will often disagree which type of beater is best — it seems to be a personal preference — but if you can try both, you will see which movement suits you best. Countermarch and counterbalanced loom manufacturers often give you a choice, with top and bottom supports that can both support a beater. The ideal position for the beater to touch the fell of the cloth, which is the last woven pick or row, is at right angles. Remember that you move the beater with each pick so comfort is very important. I have woven 6000 picks in one day, so this ease of use is very important.

Overslung: These are suspended from the top of the loom, in front of the shafts. There are usually 2–4 notches in the support so you can change the position of the beater so it always beats the cloth at right angles. On some looms the overslung beater is angled back when it lies at rest just in front of the shafts and is held in this position by the knuckles or thumb of the hand waiting to receive the shuttle. If the beater hangs straight down, it reduces the shed. The action required to hold the beater back and throw the shuttle becomes second nature with a bit of practice.

Other overslung beaters are pivoted in such a way that the beater hangs back without the help of your hands when you throw the shuttle.

Underslung: These are pivoted from the lower loom sides. Again there are usually 2–4 positions so the beater can be moved to get the correct right angle. Often the beater can also be moved up or down to raise or lower the warp threads so they remain in the centre of the reed while at rest.

Most underslung beaters incorporate a shuttle race, a ledge of wood which guides the shuttle as it travels through the shed. The lower warp ends should rest on the race to support the shuttle on its journey. Some other loom types will also have a shuttle race.

◼ REEDS

These have fine metal slats placed in the beater to separate and evenly space the warp ends (photo 1.1, page 17). There are many sizes (the number is usually stamped on the vertical end of the reed), and most weavers will have two or three. The most common sizes are 8-dent and 10-dent. This means you can place (sley) one thread in each dent (space) of an 8-dent reed to get 8 ends per 2.5cm (1in), or two through each dent to get 16 and so on. I would suggest you start with an 8- and 10-dent reed, then acquire more as you get more experienced. For example, if you weave a lot of floor rugs you may want a 5-dent reed, or if you are into fine cloth weaving, a 15 may be more appropriate. See Appendix A, page 175, for information about different reed spacings.

Stainless steel reeds are more expensive but are worth it in the long run as they will not rust. Old rusted reeds can be cleaned, but it is rather a laborious task. You can get them glass blasted or do it yourself by running fine sheets of sandpaper between each dent, and using steel wool on the outside.

■ TREADLES FOR FLOOR LOOMS

These can be attached at the back or the front of the loom and sometimes you will be given a choice by the loom manufacturer. Again, as with over or underslung beaters, weavers have personal preferences.

On rising shed looms, the treadles are usually front-slung as this allows for greater movement of the treadles. Remember that on rising shed looms, the treadles must be depressed the height of the shed. On counterbalance and countermarch looms, the treadles need only be depressed half as much, because one layer moves down as the other moves up.

Before you make a decision on which loom to buy, sit down and work the treadles if possible, as much depends on how easy it is for you to depress them. One of my very short students couldn't reach my treadles at all. I personally prefer front-slung treadles, which are attached to a bar at the front of the loom, as I have long legs and can treadle with my feet close to the treadle ties. I also like to be able to rest my foot on the other treadles while I push down with the weaving foot. Front-slung treadles need to be set at such a height that your knees are comfortable and not bumping against the cloth roller.

Back-slung treadles are attached to a bar at the back of the loom, and they swing freely at the front. There is usually greater vertical movement with this set-up, although this can depend on the size of the loom from front to back. The deeper the loom, the longer the treadles. A bar at the lower front of the loom helps to rest your non-weaving foot.

The height of your weaving seat is important for both types of treadles. The breast beam should be at such a height that when your arms are bent at right angles at the elbow, they just skim the breast beam.

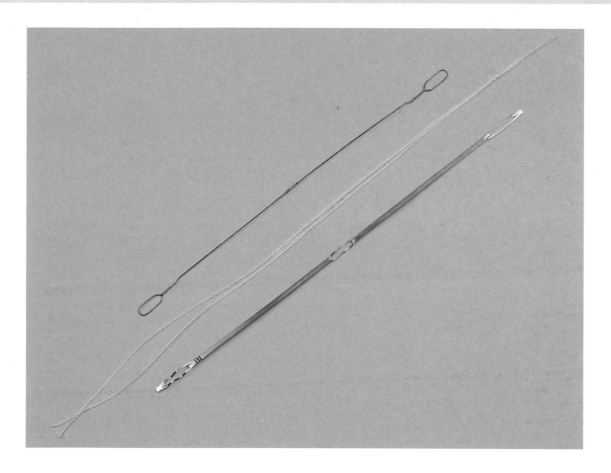

◼ HEDDLES

When I bought my first loom, I tied my own heddles as I saved $15, a considerable amount in 1973. It was a chore, but came in useful later on when I wanted to put in a replacement heddle when I made a threading mistake. There are three main types of heddles.

1.2 Heddles, from top: wire, Texsolv and flat steel

Texsolv heddles:
- If you purchase these and place them on the loom yourself, they will be joined together and will need cutting apart. Do this after placing them on the shafts.
- Are made of strong polyester, with a ladder-like construction, which leaves a rectangular gap to put the warp end through.
- Do not stretch and are light and flexible.
- Are easy to colour with spirit-based pens, so you can differentiate between shafts when threading.
- Are usually used on looms where metal heddles can be too heavy, such as multi-shaft looms. A 16-shaft loom contains four times as many heddles as a 4-shaft loom.
- Come in various sizes.

How many shafts should you begin with?

I wove with four shafts for many years before I began to want more, in fact you could weave for a lifetime with just four shafts. I began with a 4-shaft table loom, then progressed to a 4-shaft countermarch floor loom, then to a 16-shaft computer-assisted dobby loom. That step was a big leap into the unknown. Now I have 24 shafts!

If you need a loom to take to workshops, a table loom or a small portable jack loom are best. I would recommend a 4-shaft loom that has the option of adding another four later on.

- Are quiet when weaving.
- Are easy on the warp threads.
- Are not as easy to move along the shafts as other types.
- Are usually used on shafts that have no side supports.

Flat steel heddles

- Move easily along the shafts.
- Because they are angled, they fit into each other and take up less room than other heddles when pushed together.
- Are heavier, so often used on jack looms, which use gravity to drop the shafts.
- Noisier than other heddles when weaving.
- More expensive than other types.
- Usually made for shafts which have side supports to the frames.
- The eyes should all be slanted in the same direction.

Wire heddles

- Lighter than flat steel heddles.
- Bend more easily than flat steel and can get twisted around each other.
- Usually cost less than other heddles.
- Usually made for shafts that have side supports to the frames.
- The eyes should be slanted in the same direction.

■ MORE COMPLEX LOOM TYPES

As a beginner, you are probably overwhelmed enough at this stage with all the varieties of looms I have already described. But I would like to tell you about the types of looms you may move on to in the future.

DOBBY LOOMS

These can be manual or computer-assisted. They work the same way as the old pianolas or self-playing pianos, if you are old enough to remember these. The advantage of this system is that the shaft combinations are not limited by the number of treadles. On a 4-shaft loom, there are 14 possible combinations. On a table loom, you can use any of these combinations. On most floor looms, because we only have two legs and the space beneath the loom is limited, there can only be 6–10 treadles.

Manual dobby: Where the pianolas had stiff paper rolls with holes punched through, these looms have a chain of bars, or lags, each of which has pegs inserted to select the shafts to be raised. Each lag represents one pick. In some books you will see 'peg plans' for the treadling tie-up; these are written for this type of loom. These lags move for each woven pick and the pegs select the shaft to rise. If the peg protrudes, the shaft rises; if there is no peg, the shaft remains stationary. The weaver pegs the lags before weaving for the complete weaving sequence. These looms only have two treadles, as the selection is done when pegging. The pick sequence can be as long as the number of lags on your loom. These looms are multi-shaft — from 8–16 is usual.

Computer-assisted dobby: These work on the same principle as the pegged dobby loom but the sequence is pre-set on the computer screen and sent to a solenoid box on the loom. This replaces the manual dobby chain with computer-controlled lifting shaft selection that allows unlimited sequences. These looms can have as many as 44 shafts, but with this number the weight of lifting many shafts at once is generally too great for just foot power alone and an e-lift, which is air-assisted, is used with the treadles.

DRAW-LOOMS

These are used for weaving complex patterns or images. They consist of the normal set of shafts, from 4–10, with long eye heddles. Behind this set is another set of pattern shafts (up to 100) attached by a draw-loom bridge and worked independently by handles. The pattern shafts hold other layers of warp. The number of shafts make these looms very long — some can be 2.4m (8ft) in length. You need a lot of room!

Warping the loom

You will learn how to thread the loom

Minimum loom width: 30cm (12in)

The first warp (the lengthwise threads) I put on my new 4-shaft loom took three days! I felt stupid and clumsy, as it all seemed so difficult and slow. I had a book with some drawings, but it had no photographs and no explanation of why I was doing these actions. I couldn't work out why I was making a cross with the threads and it took months before that action was clear to me.

It didn't help that when I bought my loom, I was asked if I wanted to buy a raddle and a warping board. I had no idea what they were talking about, money was short, so I said no. Of course when I read the instructions in the book, I knew they were necessary, so we made these vital pieces of equipment. I had no warp plan as I wasn't even sure which threads would be the warp or weft, and no idea of what I wanted the final cloth to look like.

In this book, the warp plan for the projects in the following chapters is worked out for you. But very soon you will want to design your own projects and not follow my recipes. I have designed these projects so they gradually increase in complexity and by the end of the book you will be able to plan and weave your own projects. You will also find that as you weave your way through the book, you will want to make changes, e.g. add a runner to the table mats in Chapter 7 or use the same structure to make a tea towel instead of mats. The colours you choose will be your own personal choice and you may want to change the yarn used. Each project will add to your confidence as well as your skill level. The projects are just suggestions, so don't feel afraid to make changes. I think I learnt more from my mistakes than I did from my successes.

■ WHAT YOU WILL NEED, APART FROM YOUR LOOM

WARPING BOARD

This makes the warp by winding the threads around pegs set into a base. A warping board with pegs a metre (if you are familiar with metrics) or a yard (if you use imperial measurements) apart helps with the planning process. The pegs need to be anchored firmly in the frame; if they bend under pressure, the warp ends will be different lengths. You can also make a warp using a warping mill like the one shown in photo 2.42, page 61.

2.1 Warping board

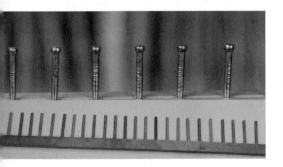

2.2 Raddle

RADDLE

This spaces the warp as you wind it onto the loom. You can make one by hammering 4cm (1½in) nails with flat heads into a flat piece of wood the same width as the reed. You can also use screw eyes instead, making sure the eyes are lined up so the threads will pass between the eyes, not through them. Many looms come with their own raddles. The pegs, nails or screw eyes can be 2.5cm (1in) apart, as in photo 2.2, 1.25cm (½in) or 0.6cm (¼in) apart.

You will also need:
- 2 large rubber bands
- 2 cross sticks: smooth lengths of wood the width of the loom, with small holes at each end. These usually come with your loom.
- Threading hook: photo 2.26, page 50
- Reed hook: photos 2.31 and 2.32, page 53
- Yarns: I have used common yarns in the projects. With the internet, it is easy to buy yarns from all over the world. Also weaving magazines advertise many shops that sell a wide variety of yarns (Appendix D, page 182).

WARP PLAN

A warp plan is the decision-making exercise you do before putting the warp on the loom. Plans look a bit daunting at first, but I will do all this for you. Warp plans focus you on the vital decisions you need to make before you actually make the warp.

- What is the finished article going to be?
- What yarn to use in the warp (lengthwise) and weft (widthwise) threads)?
- How long will the warp be?
- How wide will the warp be?
- What structure will I be weaving?

There are many ways to warp, depending on the dexterity of the weaver and the type of loom and equipment. In the following pages, I will use a tried and true method of warping that I use for all my beginner students: taking the warp from the back of the loom to the front. At the end of the chapter, I will discuss other methods. This back-to-front method is suitable for both floor and table looms. I also tell my students to use this one method until they are absolutely familiar with it before they try other methods. Too much different advice at the beginning is confusing.

■ STARTING SIMPLE

For our first project I have chosen a scarf as this is a simple project to plan and weave

Finished article: A scarf, with some added warp to allow you to sample some structures and improve the selvedges before you weave the scarf itself.

Warp and weft yarn: Medium-weight wool. Because you will be wearing this scarf next to your skin, the yarn should be soft. To test if the yarn is soft enough, rub a few strands under your chin. If you find wool irritating, choose a soft cotton instead. Generally, the looser the ply, the softer the yarn. Always choose the yarn best suited for the purpose.

Yarn wraps: To judge the correct size of yarn for this project, wind some medium-weight wool yarn around a ruler for 2.5cm (1in), without stretching it and with the yarns just touching, as in photo 2.3. Aim for 16 turns or 'wraps'. If you get less than that, the wool is too thick. If you get more than 16 turns, the yarn is too thin. Don't choose a fluffy yarn for this first project as we will cover how to deal with fluffy yarns like mohair later in the book. In each of the projects in the following chapters, I will give the size of the yarn used in m/kg (yd/lb) as well as number of wraps per 2.5cm (1in), as this means that if you can't buy exactly the same yarns I have used you can measure other yarns to get approximately the same size.

Wraps per 2.5cm (1in) is a good way to determine the warp spacing, or sett. The 16 wraps take up the same space as would 8 vertical warp ends, and 8 horizontal weft ends. So by winding with 16 wraps per 2.5cm (1in), and halving that number, we have the correct warp spacing of 8.

2.3 Correct size of yarn

Identifying types of yarn

For the projects in this book, I have suggested different yarns that would be suitable for you to use for each one, including wool, linen, cotton, mohair and many others. If you are unsure about what sort of yarn you have, doing a burn test is a useful way of helping to identify it. See Appendix C, page 181.

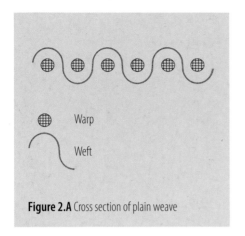

Figure 2.A Cross section of plain weave

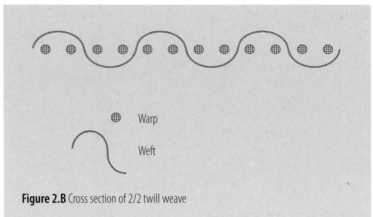

Figure 2.B Cross section of 2/2 twill weave

In Appendix B, pages 176–78, there are photos of the yarns used in each chapter. These yarns are the same size as the original so if you lay your yarn over the photographed sample, you can see how close you are. The appendix also includes the sources where you can purchase these yarns. I can't list all the sources but this will give you a start.

Length of warp: I usually weave my scarves 1.8m (6ft) long, with an 8cm (3in) fringe each end. Then we need to add wastage, which is the amount of warp used up when tying the warp onto the warp and cloth beams. If we add 1m (3ft) to our warp, this will allow for wastage. Also some yarns will shrink more when washed than others.

I have added another 1m (3ft) or so to the warp length for you to have a play before you begin weaving each project. This allows you to see any mistakes in the threading you may have missed earlier, and to get the beat correct. You will need approximately 400gm (14oz) of wool yarn for the warp and weft for this project.

Warp for 1 scarf: 2m (6½ft), including fringes
Wastage: 1m (3ft)
Sampling: 1m (3ft)
TOTAL: 4m (13ft)

Width of warp: Scarves can vary in width but a finished width of 23cm (9in) will make for a cosy scarf. There is always some pull-in at the sides so to allow for this and for shrinkage when washed, make the warp 25cm (10in) wide.

Sett: This is the number of warp ends per centimetre (inch). It varies for different structures. Plain weave, where the weft goes over and under alternate warp ends, is sett further apart than a twill structure, where the warp crosses over more than one warp end at a time. As this is a practice warp, we will use the same sett for both these structures on this first warp.

For this yarn we will use a sett of 8 ends per 2.5cm (8 ends per 1in). This is usually shortened to e.p.2.5cm (1in). I counted 16 turns when I wound the wool around the ruler for 2.5cm (1in), as in photo 2.3, page 37, so halve this number for the correct sett because half will be warp and half will be weft.

The abbreviations e.p.i and e.p.2.5cm are used frequently: e.p.i = ends per inch and e.p.2.5cm = ends per 2.5cm. Remember that one inch is approximately the same as 2.5cm.

WINDING THE WARP

Set up the warping board. Ideally, I like my board to hang on the wall with the top and lower edges at a good height for my arms to reach. If this is not possible, rest it on a table or chair. A warping mill (photo 2.42, page 61) can also be used for winding the warp.

Cones of yarn are easier to wind from than balls. If the yarn is in hanks, wind it into a ball first. Place the cone on a holder on the floor. Your holder can simply be a 15cm (6in) nail hammered into a solid piece of wood. If you have a ball of yarn, place it in a container to stop it rolling around the floor. Place the cone or ball by your feet below the centre of the board and tie one end to the first peg. The warping board in the photos is 91cm (36in) across. I can work out the length required as I go around the first time. Some weavers like to measure out the warp length with a yarn in a separate colour first as a guide. It takes a while to develop a hand rhythm when warping, and at first you will feel clumsy and slow. But it is amazing how quickly you will master this skill. I hold the yarn coming straight up from the cone/ball in one hand, while the other hand makes the journey around the pegs.

If you are making a very wide warp, it is difficult to stop the yarn from slipping off the pegs, so wind two or more separate warps. For 1.20m (4ft) wide warps, I would wind four separate warps to make up the width.

2.4 Tie the end of the yarn to peg A and take it around the board as shown, dipping it up and down at pegs B and C to form the first part of a cross, to peg D at the bottom of the board. The cross simply keeps the threads in order.

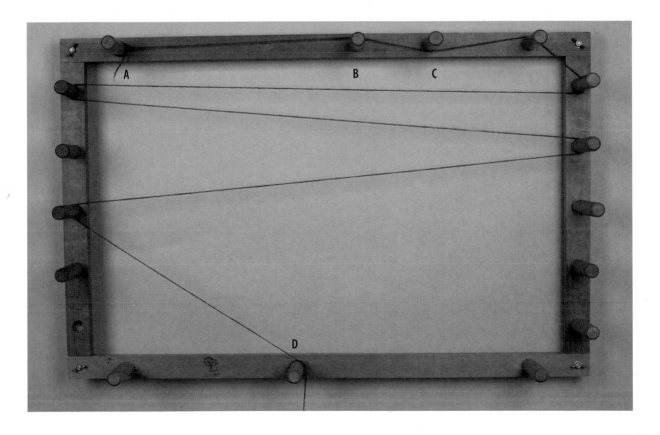

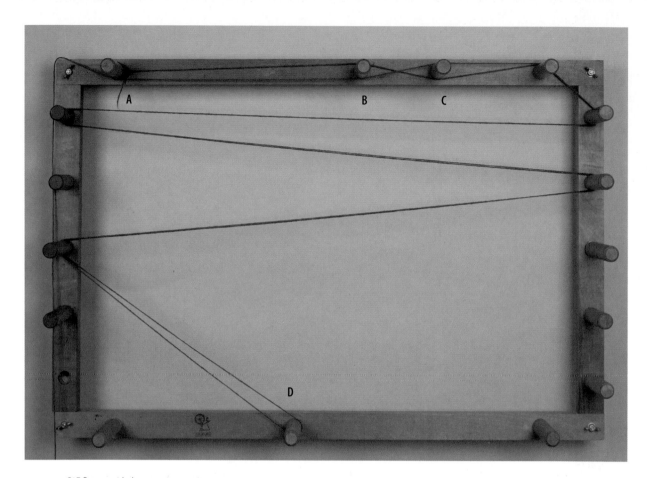

2.5 Return with the second warp end to peg A, taking the yarn over peg C and under peg B to form the second half of the cross.

2.6 Repeat this three more times until you have wound 8 threads. To reduce the amount of distance your arms stretch, from one side of the board to the other, swing your whole body as well. This helps generate a rhythm too.

2.7a Make a counting tie with a snitch knot (figure 2.C) around these 8 threads in the position shown in photo 2.8, and push the yarn down around the pegs. When I first wound my warps I didn't know about the counting ties, and if I was interrupted during the warping process I had to count from the beginning again.

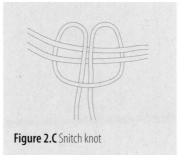

Figure 2.C Snitch knot

2.7b To maintain the tension, wind the yarn around peg A a couple of times while you make the counting tie, but do remember to unwind these turns before you wind the next eight threads.

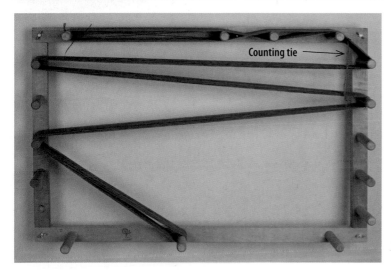

Counting tie →

2.8 Continue winding the warp until you have 80 ends and 10 counting ties. (Width 25cm (10in) multiplied by 8 ends per 2.5cm (1in)). If you have to join on a new yarn, make the join at peg A or D. Do the same if you find a knot in the yarn and have to break the yarn and rejoin it.

41

2.9 Put 4 bow knots around the cross as shown at pegs B and C, as it is important you keep this cross intact when you remove the warp from the board. Also put choke ties around the warp in three places to keep it in one piece. Add a further tie at peg D. These ties should be in a different colour to make them easy to undo and to differentiate them from the warp itself.

2.10 Remove the warp from the board, starting at peg D, and chaining as you go. Chaining just makes the warp easier to handle. If you are not putting it on the loom immediately, put the warp in a bag to prevent it getting tangled.

BEAMING

This is the process of winding the warp onto the loom. Unless you are using the beater to hold the raddle, I find it easier to remove the beater and reed for this next stage, as it gives me more room to work in.

This method of beaming is easier if you have a helper. If you are winding on by yourself, see photos 2.49–2.51, pages 66–67.

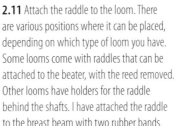

2.11 Attach the raddle to the loom. There are various positions where it can be placed, depending on which type of loom you have. Some looms come with raddles that can be attached to the beater, with the reed removed. Other looms have holders for the raddle behind the shafts. I have attached the raddle to the breast beam with two rubber bands.

2.12 Remove all the ties from the rod attached to the warp beam except for one tie at one end. Put the warp loop that was at peg A, the end nearest the counting ties, through the back rod then reattach the tie at the other end. (Some looms have a cloth apron which attaches the back rod to the warp beam instead of string ties.) Leave the other ties until the warp is correctly spaced in the raddle. Make sure the first and last ends are looped onto the rod with the rest of the warp. Take the warp through the shafts (you may need to push the heddles to both sides) and over the raddle and breast beam.

2.13 On most looms there is nothing to support the cross sticks, which you'll use in the next step. Attach loops of string to the castle with a snitch knot as shown, with a loop at each end of the string. One loop should be slightly higher than the other and about level with the heddle eyes.

2.14 Put the cross sticks through the cross in the warp and then through the string loops. The back stick should be about 2.5cm (1in) higher than the front stick. This makes it easier to see the crossed ends when threading the heddles. The cross sticks must be very smooth as any rough edges will catch on the warp ends as you roll the warp on. Join the cross sticks loosely together. I use shoelaces for this. Not only do the cross sticks keep the ends in order, they also add and even out the tension as you wind the warp on.

2.15 Remove the cross ties.

2.16 Each group of ends, secured by the counting ties, contains 8 ends. Measure 12cm (5in) from the centre of the raddle, undo the first counting tie and place those first 8 ends in the correct raddle space. If your raddle has spaces every 1.25cm (½in), put 4 ends in each space. If your raddle has 0.6cm (¼in) spaces, put 2 ends in each space. I usually put a folded piece of paper over the raddle to stop the ends falling through before they are placed in the raddle.

2.17 Place all the ends in the raddle in the right order and secure them in place. If you have lost the counting ties, the warp ends as they go alternately over and under the cross sticks will give you the correct order. If you have screw eyes in your raddle, a thin metal rod can be put through all the eyes to secure the warp ends. If you have nails or pegs, use large rubber bands stretched over the pegs or nails. Some more fancy raddles have a raddle cap for this purpose. Those raddles that fit into the beater can be secured by replacing the top beater cap.

2.18 Go to the back of the loom, and spread the warp ends out over the back rod so they line up approximately with the raddled ends. Then reattach all the ties from the back beam to the rod. If you don't do this, the rod may bow under pressure when you weave near the end of the warp, creating tension differences.

Now you are ready to roll the warp on. This is easier with two people, but I will explain how to wind the warp on your own later in this chapter.

At the back of the loom, have something ready to separate the warp ends as they are wound on the warp beam. If you don't have these separators and the warp is wound on too loosely, the warp ends will fall through the layers and you will have a spongy feel to the warp on the warp beam and an uneven tension as you weave. The aim is to wind on all the warp ends so they are equal in tension and will remain so when weaving.

If the warp ends stick together or catch on the cross sticks and a tug or shake doesn't help, a gentle comb through with the fingers can do the trick. If you have one end looser than the others, lift this end out of the warp and hold it in your hand under the same tension as the rest of the warp.

Remove the choke ties when you come to them. Make sure the warp is held in a straight line and at some distance from the raddle. If you hold it tighter on one side than the other, you will end up with a 'banana' shaped warp as you weave. If you hold the warp too close to the raddle, the angle is too great and the centre ends will be at a different tension than the outside ends.

2.19 The separators for the warp beam should be wider than the warp. Thin sticks, a roll of wallpaper, a roll of strong brown paper, venetian blind slats, or corrugated cardboard (with the smooth side uppermost) are suitable.

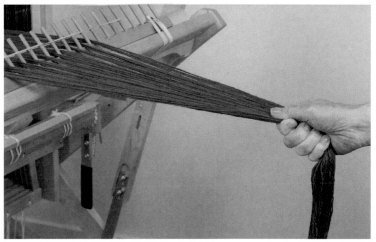

2.20 The person at the front of the loom holds the warp tight. As this is a narrow warp, it can be held in one hand. For a wider warp use two hands but make sure you apply the same pressure with both hands. Give the warp a good shake and tug every now and then to separate the ends. The basic idea is that the warp should not be handled too much while winding on as this can cause tension problems. A tensioned warp should not tangle.

2.21 The person at the back of the loom turns the handle to wind on the warp, and also places the separators in between each layer. If using sticks or slats, the first separator goes in to cover the knots in the string ties, and then in each subsequent round, placing each slat just past the previous one so there is no build-up. If using paper, insert the paper over the first knots, making sure it is straight. If it is not straight, the paper will roll on unevenly and eventually the edge of the warp falls off the paper and you have to unwind and begin again. Make sure the warp does not fall off the separators, which should be at least 5cm (2in) wider than the warp width.

47

2.22 Check you are turning the handle the right way. If you have a ratchet and pawl system, when you stop winding, the pawl should engage the ratchet and prevent it unwinding. In one of my classes we wound on a 9m (29½ft) warp the wrong way and had to unwind and do it all over again. You will notice as the warp winds on that it is moving through the cross sticks so the cross will end up at the other end of the warp, ready for threading.

2.23 If you have a friction brake, make sure it is engaged so the warp beam is stationary.

2.24 When the end of the warp is about 30–40cm (12–16in) in front of the raddle, cut through the loop tie which was at peg D, separate the warp into two halves, remove the warp from the raddle and take the raddle out of the loom. Its work is now done.

2.25 Tie each half of the warp in a slip knot and leave the warp hanging between the cross sticks and the back of the shafts.

Figure 2.D Slip knot

49

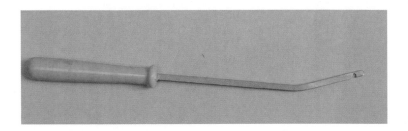

2.26 Threading hook

THREADING THE HEDDLES
Threading from the back of the loom
On one of my larger looms, I can sit on a low stool between the back beam and the shafts, and thread from the back. The only thing is that it is a bit of a scramble to get out of the loom if the phone rings! When threading this way I use the claw method (photo 2.28a).

Threading from the front of the loom
If I can comfortably reach the warp on the cross sticks, I thread sitting at the front of the loom. Adjust your chair or stool so it is the correct height. You need to see the warp cross at the cross sticks. If you can't see the cross sticks, it may help to raise all the shafts or lower your seat. If you can remove the breast beam, the beater and the reed you will have more room.

Sometimes I use a threading hook (catching the warp end in the hook and pulling the hook and end through the heddle eye) and sometimes I am quicker using my fingers, so try both. If you have an 8-shaft loom, as I have in the photographs, notice that I am just threading the first four shafts.

2.27a (right) Push 10 heddles from each shaft from the right-hand side to the centre of the shafts. I try to keep the same number of heddles at each side of the loom, as the weight distribution is then even. As there are 80 warp ends to this warp, we will need a quarter or 20 ends on each of the four shafts.

2.27b (far right) To make threading easier, it is a good idea to mark the shafts in some way. Texsolv heddles can be marked with a spirit-based pen around the eyes, as here where they are colour-coded. Or you can number the lower shaft bars.

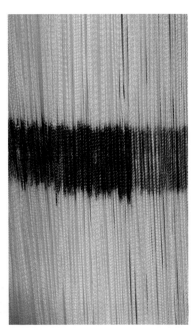

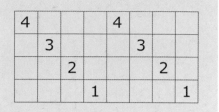

Figure 2.E Four-shaft threading draft

2.28a The draft (figure 2.E) is read from right to left, so start threading from the right-hand side. Shaft 1 is the shaft nearest to you when you are sitting at the front of the loom. (If you are reading Scandinavian threading drafts, shaft 1 is at the back of the loom.) Take the first 4 heddles from the centre group, one from each of the four shafts, and separate them from the other heddles. Take the first 4 ends from the cross, which is at eye height as I am sitting low down and place these 4 ends in the gaps between each finger and thumb, and thread from this. This 'claw' method of threading heddles is very useful as it is very hard to make a mistake. The threading draft can be marked off in fours too, which is a great help for more complex patterns.

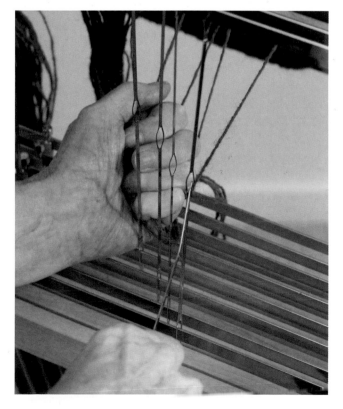

2. 28b Take the first warp end from the cross sticks and put it through the heddle eye on the first shaft.

51

2.29 Thread the next end through shaft 2, the next through shaft 3, then 4. Make sure the ends are not crossed over, e.g. the thread on shaft 2 should be in the heddle eye between shaft 1 and 3. Thread the next four shafts, check the ends are in the right places, then tie these eight ends in a slip knot (figure 2.D, page 49). Checking now saves time later on, as a mistake means you may have to undo, then redo the complete sequence, and mistakes always seem to be in the centre of the warp, making it slow to fix.

2.30 Continue threading, first moving the four heddles across, then threading them. When you reach the centre, just continue threading with the heddles from the left side of the loom. You don't need to count them out or move them to the centre. When finished, you should have 10 slip knots.

SLEYING THE REED

If you have removed the reed and/or beater, place them back in the loom. As there are 8 e.p.2.5cm (1in), an 8-dent reed is best, as you will put one warp end in each slot. If you have a reed other than an 8, see the chart in Appendix A, page 175, to determine how many warp ends to put in each space (dent).

Fix the reed in an upright position. Some looms have pegs which will do this; if your loom does not, tie a piece of string around the reed and the loom castle to hold the reed upright.

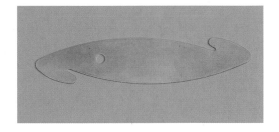

2.31 Reed hook

2.32 Measure 12cm (5in) from the centre of your reed. As this warp is 25cm (10in) wide, we need half each side of the centre. A permanent mark in the reed centre is useful. Undo the slip knot and, using the reed hook, place the very first warp end on the right side of the warp through the dent in the reed 12cm (5in) from the right of the central reed mark.

2.33 (below) Continue sleying all the warp, stopping to check now and then and tying these checked ends in a slip knot.

TYING ONTO THE CLOTH BEAM

Replace the breast beam if you removed it earlier. The rod attached to the cloth beam comes over the top of the breast beam from the front. Remove the cross sticks from the warp at the back of the loom.

Once you have tied all the knots, you are nearly ready to weave. Tighten the warp at the front ratchet and pawl until it feels firm.

TIE-UP
Table looms

As each handle is directly connected to the shafts, there is no tie-up needed. Just check that the cords that attach the shafts to the handles are correctly aligned.

2.34 Beginning in the centre of the warp, undo the slip knot and take about 4–6 warp ends and pull them tight. Pass the ends over, then under, the front rod and, dividing them in two, bring each half up both sides of the warp group and tie them around the rod as shown (Figure 2.F). This surgeon's knot is the same as the first half of a granny or reef knot, but with an extra twist. That extra twist holds the yarn firmly. About 12–15cm (5–6in) is enough yarn for this knot, as you don't want to waste too much warp at this stage.

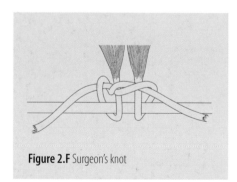

Figure 2.F Surgeon's knot

2.35 Working from the centre out, complete all the knots, then test the warp is all the same tension by running the back of your hand over the warp. You will usually find the centre knots need tightening by pulling on the warp tails. The beauty of this surgeon's knot is that it is so easy to adjust the tension. Do not complete the knot with a bow or another turn at this stage.

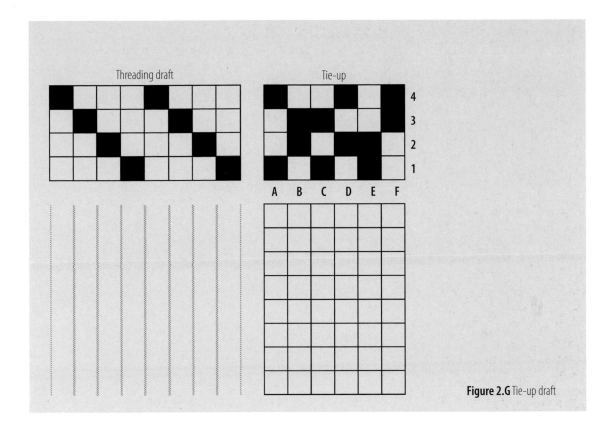

Figure 2.G Tie-up draft

Floor looms

Plain weave and 2/2 twill are the most common weave structures
and the ones you will use for the first few projects, so it makes sense
to tie up your floor loom now for these structures. You need to tie
the correct shafts to each treadle before you start weaving. Different
looms have different methods of connecting the shafts to the loom;
some have lamms (figure 1.B, page 19) which connect the shafts
to the treadles. Sometimes the ties are string, sometimes Texsolv
(a special nylon cord) and some looms have hooks, so follow the
instructions for your loom.

The tie-up instructions are in the top right quadrant of the draft
and are for six treadles. In the tie-up in figure 2.G, the centre two
treadles are tied up for plain weave. The shafts in use are indicated
by the black squares. So for plain weave, the left-hand centre treadle
(C) will lift 1 & 3 and the right-hand centre treadle (D) 2 & 4. The
remaining treadles are tied up for the twill weaving structure: 1 & 2, 2
& 3, 3 & 4, 4 & 1 (more about this structure later). I use a 'walking the
treadles' tie-up for the twill structure. This means I use the left and
right feet alternately, as in walking.

Sometimes it helps to label the treadles A, B, C, D E, F, from left to
right, on both the draft and your loom. Then to lift shafts 1 & 3, you
depress treadle C and for shafts 2 & 4, you depress treadle D.

WEAVING THE HEADING

The heading will fill in the gaps left by the knots and will also show up any mistakes or tension differences. Use thick waste wool in a contrasting colour for this. I have seen many things used as headers at this stage, old nylon stockings seem to be a favourite for many but I find they take up too much warp and leave large bumps.

2.36 Wind a few turns of waste wool around a stick shuttle (photo 3.1, page 71), then weave one pick (row) through the shed made by lifting shafts 1 & 3. Beat this into place, close to the knots, then weave 3 more picks, without beating, just changing the shafts, the next pick being 2 & 4, then 1 & 3 again, then 2 & 4. Beat these 3 picks with several firm taps of the beater. Leaving little loops at the selvedges makes it easier to remove the heading later. You may need to repeat these 3 picks once more to close up the warp gaps.

2.37 If there are loose spots, tighten the knot by pulling on the warp tails. If one knot is looser than the others, the warp will bulge up at this point. If it is tighter, it will sink down.

CHECKING FOR MISTAKES
Check the threading and **sleying** are correct.

Sleying mistakes
If you missed a dent in the reed, there will be a gap. If you put 2 ends through one dent instead of one, they will be crammed together.

> Sleying: Bringing the warp end through the reed.

2.38 To fix mistakes in the sleying, you will need to re-sley from this point. You don't need to remove all the ends from the reed to do this. If you have missed a gap, just move each warp end over one space as shown. If you have spaced two in one dent, move one over from the nearest side until you come to the doubled end.

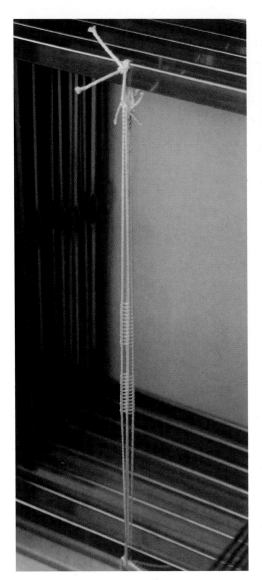

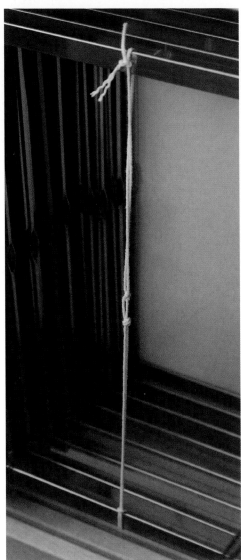

2.39 If your loom uses Texsolv heddles, or you have any spare Texsolv heddles the same size as your metal ones, take two heddles. Loop them through each other with a snitch knot so they are joined at one end. Place the looped heddles under the lower shaft 3 bar, bring the heddles past each side of the upper shaft 3 bar and join them with a string tie. When you thread these replacement heddles, make sure the warp end goes through both heddle eyes, as this prevents the heddles slipping.

2.40 You can also make a replacement string heddle. Take a doubled length of fine string, place the loop around the lower shaft bar, on shaft 3, between shafts 2 and 4, and up to the top of the heddle bar. Now comes the tricky bit. Two people are sometimes better than one at doing this bit. Tie an overhand knot in the doubled length at exactly the same place as the lower point of the adjacent heddle eyes. Sometimes I get the helper to hold a pencil on top of this first knot to make the eye. Now tie another knot to match the upper point of the adjacent heddle eye, then take the two lengths and knot them together over the top of the heddle bar. Tie and re-tie if necessary until you get it spot on. If the string eye isn't the same level as the other heddle eyes, the end in that eye will be out of line in the shed.

Threading mistakes

This depends on what the mistake is. For example, if you have threaded 1, 2, 2, 4 instead of 1, 2, 3, 4, you can make a replacement heddle for shaft 3.

One end missed out in the heddles and reed

This is the slowest mistake to fix. When I first began weaving I would remove all the threads up to this point from the reed and heddles and re-do the whole process. This would take hours. Now I have a quicker method.

If you have threaded 1, 3, 4 and there is no spare thread, it is easy to make a replacement heddle, as in photo 2.39, on the correct shaft. Then take a length of the warp yarn, the same length as the warp length and place it in the replacement heddle.

You will have to re-sley the reed from this point to make a gap as in photo 2.38, page 57. Thread the replacement end through the correct dent, then tie one end to the front rod with the rest of the warp ends. The other end hangs over the back beam and is weighted to make it the same tension as the rest of the warp. If the warp is very long, I wind this replacement yarn into a small ball and suspend a weight from the ball. See page 143 for suitable weighting devices. You will have to move the weight down when you advance the warp.

Crossed ends between the shaft and the reed

This is because you have a different order from the shafts to the reed. When you sleyed the reed, you may have them as 1, 3, 2, 4, instead of 1, 2, 3, 4.

2.41 This is easy to fix. Just remove the 2 crossed ends and re-sley them. It is easier to see these crossed ends if you open the shed and look through from the side.

■ OTHER WAYS OF DOING THINGS

Earlier in this chapter, I asked you to wind and put on a warp according to my instructions. There are lots of other ways to do this — every experienced weaver will have their own favourite way. Also much depends on the type of loom you have and your dexterity and mobility. Once you have put on a few warps and can understand the reasons why you are doing things my way, read through the following section, which will explain other methods you may like to try.

WARPING MILL

This is an alternative piece of equipment to a warping board. It is sometimes called a warping reel. There are two types: vertical (photo 2.42) and horizontal. The vertical mill takes up less room while winding, but the warp has a tendency to fall down the mill as you remove it when chaining. The pegs which make up the cross can be moved to various positions, depending on the length of warp needed.

Advantages

- Can make a much longer warp, 35m (38yd) or more.
- Less strain on your arms as you are not reaching from peg to peg.
- The uprights of the mill take the strain of the warp ends, so you should not have the end of the warp much longer than the beginning. On a warping board, if the pegs angle even slightly under the pressure of the warp, the warp becomes shorter at the end. On the mill you still need to make several warps if you are winding a wide warp as the build-up of the threads causes the ends nearest to the uprights to be shorter than the outside ends.
- Takes less time to wind a warp

Disadvantages

- More expensive than a warping board.
- Takes up more room. However, they are usually collapsible, and can be hung on a peg when not in use. I had a mill with a heck block (a system which mechanically spreads the warp at exact intervals around the mill. The heck block has a heddle-like piece attached which enables you to wind several threads at once and make a cross in them) and although it was a very efficient and quick way to wind warps for production weaving, it was not collapsible and took up a lot of room.

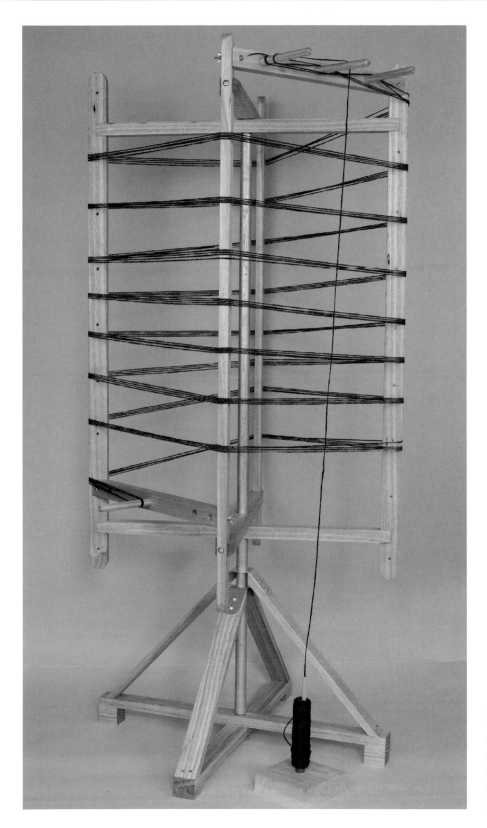

2.42 Vertical warping mill. This mill has 16.5m (54ft) wound on. When warping with two crosses (photo 2.44, page 63), two more pegs are added to the lower peg rail.

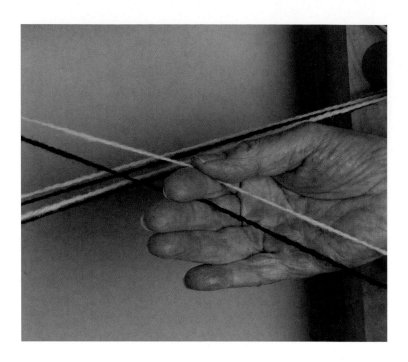

2.43 Winding with two warp ends.

WINDING WITH TWO WARP ENDS AT ONCE

This speeds up warping considerably and I use it a lot, especially with fine threads. Knot two ends of the warp yarn together, slip this loop over peg A and wind the warp as usual. You **must** separate the two ends between your fingers as you wind, otherwise they will twist around each other as you weave, the warp won't go through the heddles and the twist will build up until it is impossible to advance the warp. Of course, if you are threading these two warp threads as one end through the heddles and reed to get the right thickness, this will not matter and there is no need to separate them.

When you come to the cross while threading, you will have two warp ends over the cross sticks and two under. Just take any one of this pair while threading, then the second end. If you are following a certain colour order, it will be necessary to maintain this order when threading.

WINDING WITH TWO CROSSES

This is necessary when using fluffy yarns that will stick or yarns that are sett very close together and will not move over the cross sticks when you are beaming the warp. By putting a cross at each end of the warp, you can keep the raddle cross at one end of the warp, and the threading cross at the other end. This means you don't run the warp through the cross sticks.

I also use this method when I am winding long warps of over about 12m (13yd) as it saves time. In photo 2.44 you can see my ingenious method of supporting the warping board as I wind. The height is such that I can sit down to warp. Step ladders have lots of uses!

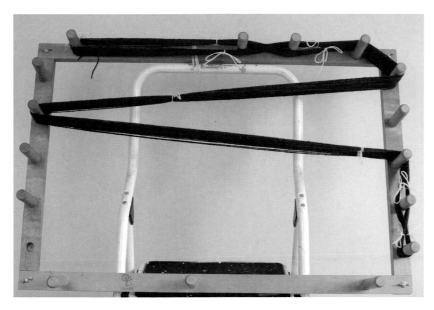

2.44 Wind the warp with two crosses as shown, adding the counting ties. Put ties around both crosses as usual, then chain the warp as normal.

2.45 Attach the warp end with the counting ties to the back rod (as in photo 2.12, page 43), but instead of placing the cross sticks through that cross, tie a length of string to the back rod, through the second part of the cross, and attach the other end of the string to the back rod at the other end. This keeps the cross intact in case you lose it when you are placing the warp in the raddle. Undo the cross ties at that end of the warp.

Follow the instructions in photos 2.16–2.23, pages 45–48, to beam the warp, only this time the ends do not travel over and under the cross stick. This makes for easy rolling on, but remember to still add the separators between each layer.

2.46 When the end of the warp is about 50cm (20in) from the raddle, remove the ends from the raddle, place a cross stick through the warp in the section of the cross nearest to the shafts and work this stick back behind the shafts. You may need to jiggle the stick and separate the warp ends to move the cross back. Remember, yarn under tension tangles least, so hold the warp under some tension as you do this. Push down the lower layer a few threads at a time as you move the cross back.

It is safer to leave the cross ties in as you move the cross back behind the shafts. However, with sticky warps, the threads won't move until the cross ties are removed and the warp can spread out more. If you do remove the cross ties, do not remove all four at once. Just take out one set at a time. Once the ties are removed, the only thing keeping the cross in place is your hands!

2.47 Place the first cross stick in the higher loops of the string you have prepared to hold the sticks (photos 2.13 and 2.14, page 44).

2.48 Undo the first two cross ties and place the second cross stick in the front part of the cross and work this cross and stick back behind the shafts. Again, a bit of jiggling and separating the ends is usually necessary. Place this second cross stick in the lower string loop and tie the cross sticks together. When all this is done, cut through the end of the warp and you are ready to begin threading.

BEAMING A WARP ON YOUR OWN
For table looms or narrow floor looms
Method A: Warp as described in photos 2.11–2.19, pages 43–47. If you can reach far enough, you can hold the warp firmly at the front with one hand while the other hand turns the ratchet and places the separators. Remember to stop to shake and tug the warp at intervals and make sure the warp is held in a direct line, not pulled to one side.
Method B: Warp as described in photos 2.11–2.19. Then tension each **bout** at the front of the loom.

A **bout** is a group of warp ends.

2.49 Grasp the warp, give it a good shake and tug, then leave it loose on the floor at the front of the loom.

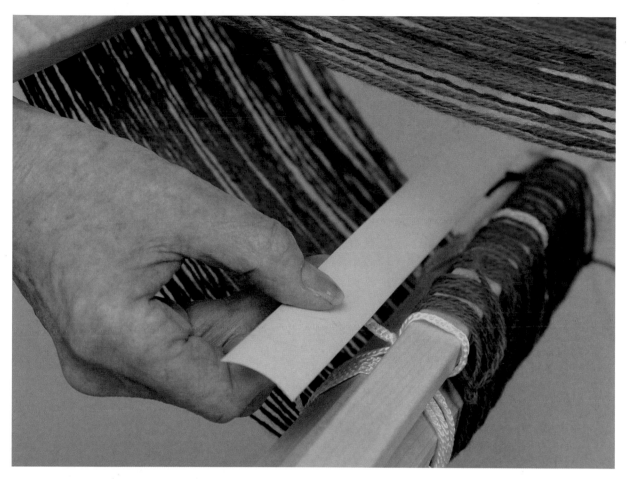

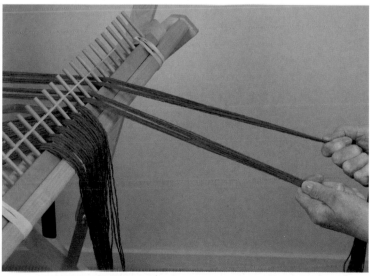

2.50 Wind one full turn of the warp around the warp beam, with a slat or two inserted to cover the knots. Slats or sticks are much better for this method than paper separators. Don't worry that the warp is not under tension around the warp beam at this stage.

2.51 Go to the front of the loom. Take the warp and separate it into about 5cm (2in) bouts, and give each bout a good firm pull, holding it beyond the raddle. I rock myself back on my heels while doing this, so my full body weight is behind each tug, as this will give each bout an even tension. You will notice how the warp tightens all the way around the warp beam.

Continue winding on the loose warp for one complete turn, tugging each bout, then placing in another stick or slat. You can see why we need to use sticks or slats, as you need to be able to see exactly when the warp beam has done one complete turn, no more or less. The warp will only tighten around that one turn; once one layer has passed over the last, the warp cannot be tightened.

When the warp is near the end, follow the instructions from photo 2.22, page 48.

WARPING FRONT TO BACK

This seems to be a method of warping the loom that is mainly used in the United States. The warp is wound on a warping board as usual, then taken to the front of the loom, cross sticks are placed in the cross, the loop at peg A is cut, and the ends are then threaded through the reed and heddles in the correct order. The warp is tied onto the back rod, then wound onto the warp beam. There is no need for a raddle, as the ends are spaced by the reed and heddles while being wound on. I have only tried this method twice and I found the following:

- Because the ends at peg A have to be cut before placing them in the reed, I had to make sure they stayed on the cross sticks and I didn't lose the cross.
- When I tied the ends onto the back rod, I couldn't get them exactly the same length and the resulting difference in tension made the warp slightly tangled as I wound on. I had to comb it with my fingers to equalise the tension and once I started this I had to do this all the way through the warp as I wound on.
- The knots on the warp beam had to be covered with slats or sticks to prevent them upsetting the tension.
- The warp had to be wound through the heddles and reed twice: once while beaming and once while weaving. This puts a strain on the warp. For delicate warp threads, this could result in broken ends.

I am sure if I had practised this method more I would have improved my technique. One of my pet theories is that the less the warp is handled after it comes off the warping board, the easier it is to wind on, as the tension has not changed. When winding front to back, the warp is handled much more and some of the original tension is usually lost. As all weavers have different abilities, body shapes, types of looms and levels of dexterity, there will always be many different methods of doing things, and you will soon find what suits you and your needs best.

SECTIONAL WARPING

I will just describe this briefly here as I think a beginner would need some experience and specialised equipment, making this method more suitable for experienced weavers who wind long, wide warps.

A sectional back beam has wooden or metal pegs spaced every

2.5cm (1in) or 5cm (2in) apart and replaces the warp beam. The warp is wound directly from spools or cones, one spool or cone for each warp end, onto each section of the beam. If you can buy these yarn packages already wound, you can save time, but if you have to wind these spools or cones yourself, it can be tedious.

The spools or cones are placed on a spool holder (creel) directly behind the loom, the threads go through a tension box, then are wound on to each section of the beam. For a sectional beam with 2.5cm (1in) spaces, you would need 16 spools if you are threading 16 ends per 2.5cm (1in). Once one space has the correct length of warp on, a cross is made and the ends are cut. The tension box and creel are moved to the next space and the next 2.5cm (1in) is wound on. A counter is needed to make sure each section has the same number of turns. The tension box equalises the tension on each end.

TYING A NEW WARP ONTO THE OLD

This sounds good to a beginner because it eliminates the threading of the heddles and the reed for a new warp, but it is only possible when you have the same pattern and number of threads. A weaving friend of mine wove many mohair scarves for a shop, and kept one loom for this purpose, just tying each new warp onto the old but I would not recommend it for a beginner. The only way to become quick and efficient at warping and beaming is to practise, and in the beginning you need to put on several shorter warps, using different yarns and setts.

Weaving

3

You will learn basic weaving techniques

Minimum loom width: 30cm (12in)

This is the part you have been waiting for. Before you begin weaving your scarf, you will weave a sample at the beginning of the warp so you become familiar with the loom and the action of throwing the shuttle. Choose some weft yarn about the same thickness as the warp but in a contrasting colour which will show the weave structures. Wind this yarn around the shuttle.

SHUTTLE TYPES

There are various types of shuttles. Beginners usually start with stick shuttles. (Photo 3.1)

STICK SHUTTLES

Shuttles of type A are flat pieces of wood with grooves and curves at both ends. Do not overfill as the shuttle will then take up too much room in the shed. Winding the weft yarn onto the shuttle in a figure of eight allows more yarn to be carried without a large build-up (photo 3.1). However, shuttles wound this way will not run as smoothly through the shed. Make sure the shuttle is smooth so it won't catch on the yarn.

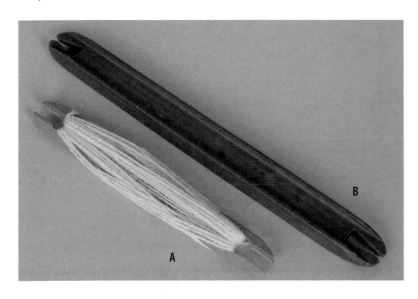

3.1 Stick shuttles (A) (B)

71

Advantages
- The simplest, least expensive shuttles, which you can make yourself.
- Because of the low cost you can have many different shuttles of varying lengths. When weaving, choose a shuttle that is slightly longer than the weaving width.
- No extra equipment, such as a bobbin winder, is necessary to wind the weft onto the shuttle.
- Can hold quite a lot of yarn so are suitable for thicker yarns.

Disadvantages
- When these shuttles are pushed though the shed, the yarn rubs against the warp ends, and there is some friction.
- To unwind the weft yarn for each pick, it may be necessary to reverse the shuttle, which slows you down and makes it harder to get a good weaving rhythm. If the shuttle is slightly longer than the weaving width it is possible, with some practice, to flick the yarn off the shuttle at the beginning of each weaving pick to allow enough to unwind for the next pick. This way you won't have to reverse the shuttle.
- The ends curve upwards but as they are flat, they can only curve in one direction, unlike B-type shuttles. Therefore it is easy to catch a stray warp end when pushing it through the shed.
- You cannot 'throw' a stick shuttle, because it doesn't glide through the shed as other types of shuttles do.
- You will need many different shuttle widths. It is best to have shuttles long enough so that the shuttle protrudes slightly from the selvedge, so you can catch it ready for the next pick. If you have to insert your fingers into the selvedge to pull the shuttle out each time, the selvedge ends will gradually become loose.

The second type of shuttle shown (B) is almost the same as the stick shuttle but it has raised edges. This is sometimes called a rag shuttle. Don't wind on so much weft that the yarn extends above the wooden sides and don't wind on with a figure of eight. These shuttles are similar to the larger rug shuttle in design.

Advantages
- Glides through the shed easily as the yarn is not in contact with the warp ends. If they are made correctly, both ends are curved upwards and inwards so they won't catch on the warp in the shed.
- Less expensive than boat and end delivery shuttles.
- Because they glide easily through the shed, they can be thrown quite wide distances. I can throw one of these shuttles acoss a warp that is twice as wide as the shuttle.

Disadvantages
- To unwind the weft when weaving, it may be necessary to reverse the shuttle, as with the A-type stick shuttle.

3.2 Rug shuttle

RUG SHUTTLES

These are used for thick yarns when weaving floor rugs, hence the name. They usually come in longer lengths than the stick shuttles, and are hollow in construction to make them lighter. They are also called rag shuttles as they are used when weaving with rag strips.

Advantages
- Will hold a lot of thick yarn.
- The raised wooden edges allow the shuttle to slide easily through the shed, so it can be thrown further than the actual weaving width.

Disadvantages
- If filled with too much yarn, they are heavy to throw.
- Their greater height needs a larger shed than other shuttles.

SKI SHUTTLES

I use these for thicker weft yarns.

Advantages
- Glide easily through the shed and can be thrown a good distance.
- The shape, with the curved ends, means they can't pick up stray warp ends in the shed.

Disadvantages
- Cost more than the stick or rug shuttles.
- May need a larger shed because they can be bigger than other shuttles.

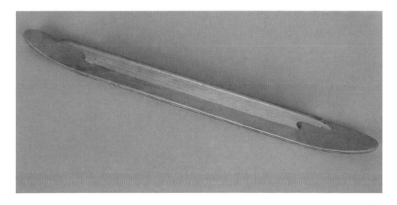

3.3 Ski shuttle

3.4 Boat shuttle and bobbin

BOAT SHUTTLES

Both boat and end delivery shuttles have the shuttle separate from the yarn holders. The weft yarn is held on a removable bobbin rotating on a central metal rod. A bobbin winder is necessary, which can be single or double ended, electric or hand operated. Boat shuttles are suitable for finer yarns and some have rollers underneath to help them glide through the shed.

To wind a bobbin for the boat shuttle, place the bobbin on the bobbin winder, wind a few turns by hand, then start the motor or turn the handle if it is a hand-operated winder. Wind the yarn on by moving your hand up and down the bobbin length, shortening each layer very slightly. When finished, the bobbin will be fatter in the centre than at the ends. As the yarn is wound on tightly, you may need a leather glove or some sort of finger protection. I have wound linen threads so tightly that the yarn almost cut into my finger. Place the wound bobbin on the metal shaft in the boat shuttle and thread the weft yarn through the slot in the side, making sure it comes out from the underside of the bobbin. The slot faces you as you throw the shuttle.

I have seen drinking straws cut into the correct length used instead of a bobbin. Paper quills (rolled tubes of paper) can be used too. These are placed onto the wire in the boat shuttle.

Advantages
- Are smaller in size but, because they move through the shed so smoothly, can be thrown long distances.
- They can be thrown across any weaving width.
- Because the weft yarn is held on a separate bobbin, you can have one shuttle with several bobbins, which can easily be interchanged when weaving with many colours or yarn types.

Disadvantages
- You will, by necessity, need extra equipment such as some sort of bobbin winder. This can be electric or handheld. I have seen many winders which are adapted from an electric drill (photo 3.6, page 76).

- More expensive than stick or rug shuttles.
- It is more difficult to wind the bobbin correctly, which requires some practice. The weft yarn must be packed tightly (see opposite page).
- The bobbin keeps on unwinding when you have completed your weft pick. To prevent too much weft unwinding, you need to place a finger or thumb on the bobbin as it comes out of the shed.
- The bobbin winds faster and with more tension when it is almost empty, and slower and with less tension when it is full, so the weft tension differs as you weave. This is controlled by the amount of weft you allow to unwind from the bobbin.

END DELIVERY SHUTTLES

These are my favourite shuttles. Again, I use them for fine yarns. The yarn holder is called a pirn: a tapered cone which is fixed between two metal points. To wind the pirn, begin by wrapping a few turns of yarn around the pirn at the larger end. Then move your hand up and down the pirn for about 2.5cm (1in), starting at the larger end and moving your hand down the pirn as you wind so each layer slightly overlaps the last. Again, you may need some sort of finger protection as the tension must be tight. Stop winding about 2.5cm (1in) from the smaller end.

Advantages

- Can be smaller in size than stick or rug shuttles because they move smoothly through the shed and can be thrown long distances.
- Can be thrown across any weaving width and the pirns can be interchanged when necessary.
- There is constant tension on the weft yarn, as the yarn is held on a stationary pirn, not a rotating bobbin as with boat shuttles.
- At one end of the shuttle there is a tension device. On the top shuttle in photo 3.5, the Bluster Bay shuttle, the tension is

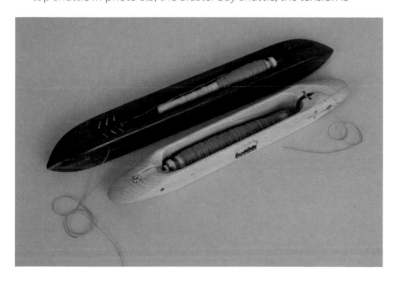

3.5 End delivery shuttles (Bluster Bay and Schacht), half-wound pirn and wound pirn

controlled by how many hooks you wind the yarn around; the more hooks the more tension. On the Schacht shuttle below it, there are jaws which can be opened or closed when adjusting the yarn tension. This means that once the tension is adjusted, the selvedges neither pull in or have little protruding loops, the tension remains constant.

Disadvantages
- Cost more than the other types of shuttles.
- Cannot hold as much yarn as stick, ski or rug shuttles so are only suitable for finer threads.
- Extra equipment is needed, such as a pirn winder and several pirns.
- Takes some practice to wind a perfect pirn.

With an electric winder, one hand is free to move up and down winding the bobbin or pirn, while the other hand can guide the yarn upwards from the yarn cone or ball. With a handheld winder, one hand must do the winding while the hand holds the winder. If you can clamp the winder to a table, this will leave both hands free.

Whatever shuttle you choose or have ended up with by default, I suggest you have a good practice at throwing it before you start weaving. Practise holding and catching it so your hand does not change position for these two movements. If you have to change, it slows you down and the weaving rhythm will be lost. Once you feel confident at handling the shuttle, you're ready to move on to a sampler. This exercise will get you used to weaving before we tackle the scarf.

3.6 Electric pirn or bobbin winder

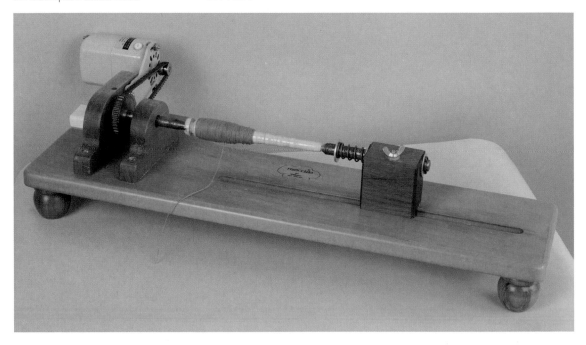

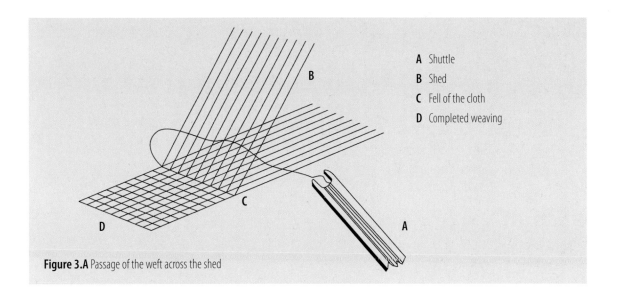

A Shuttle
B Shed
C Fell of the cloth
D Completed weaving

Figure 3.A Passage of the weft across the shed

▮ WEAVING THE SAMPLER

Weaving will feel awkward at first but you will soon become accustomed to the hand movements. With a floor loom, you will sit down to weave and this is less tiring. With some table looms, it is easier to stand to reach the handles, but try out various positions. When sitting at both floor and table looms, the front beam should be at such a height that your forearm, held at right angles to your body, just skims the breast beam. Some floor looms have an attached seat which can be adjusted to suit your height. I have an office chair which I can adjust. For threading the heddles I have the chair at the lowest position, and for weaving I move it up. This chair has a back for support.

As you should do when sitting at a computer, it is important to weave for only short spells at a time. Get up and move around every 15–30 minutes or so.

It is important to remember that the weft, when first placed across the shed, is lying in a straight line. When it is beaten against the fell of the cloth (the last weft pick), this yarn must curve over and under the warp ends to some extent. The amount the yarn bends around the warp depends on the weave structure and yarn size (figures 2.A and 2.B, page 38). A thicker yarn curves more than a thinner yarn. I didn't know this important fact when I began weaving, and my weaving pulled in 5cm (2in) each side. I couldn't pull the beater down because the edges pulled in too much, and I was very confused. Also the selvedge warp ends were under so much pressure that they kept breaking.

To allow for this pull-in, the weft must have some slack and this can be done in two ways. Bring the weft pick out of the shed higher than where it went in, as in figure 3.A, or push the centre of the weft up so it curves upwards.

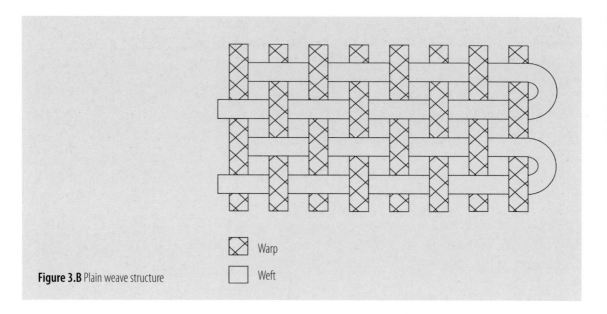

Figure 3.B Plain weave structure

☒ Warp

☐ Weft

PLAIN WEAVE

For this first project, you will use plain weave where you lift alternate warp ends. This is the most common weave and is the same structure as for the heading you did earlier. Chose a yarn the same size as the warp but a different colour as this will clearly show you the weave structure. The steps are:

1. Place the weft across the shed caused by lifting shafts 1 & 3, beginning on the right side.
2. Bring the weft out higher on the left side. Watching the outside right edge (selvedge), leave a tail of about 2.5cm (1in) hanging out. Tuck this tail in around an outside warp end and back into the shed.
3. Bring the beater up to the fell of the cloth and give a light tap of the beater with your right hand to push the weft into place. Keep your hand in the centre of the beater so the pressure is even and not to one side.
4. If you are using a floor loom, as the beater touches the fell, change into the next shed by lifting shafts 2 & 4. Then return the beater to its usual position. By changing the shed at this point you clear the shed for the next throw. It is a good habit to get into.
5. If you are using a table loom, lie the shuttle down on the weaving at the front of the loom and change into the next shed when the beater is returned. With a table loom you have to put the shuttle down to beat, so some of the rhythm is lost.

It is a good practice to watch the selvedge at the point where the shuttle enters the shed, not the point where it leaves. Then with the shuttle you can control how much to pull in. The weft yarn should be snug around the outside ends.

Do not play with the weft or pinch it at the point where it entered the shed. It is very tempting to give a little tweak here, but it is much better to control the selvedges with the shuttle rather than your fingers. Like everything else, it takes practice to get the edges right, but don't worry, that will come.

Continue weaving, lifting shafts 1 & 3, 2 & 4 alternately. Many table looms have the handles that manipulate shafts 1 & 3 on one side and 2 & 4 on the other so they can be changed together. If this is so, coordinate your hands and shuttle so that you move the handles on the same side as you enter the shuttle. Then you can pick up mistakes immediately.

For floor looms, try to coordinate your hands and feet. Push down on the right-hand treadle when the shuttle is to be thrown from the right and the left-hand treadle when the shuttle is thrown from the left. If you forget to change sheds, you will only need to undo the last weft pick and no harm is done.

If you run out of weft yarn, fill the shuttle again and overlap the last of the old yarn with about 2.5cm (1in) of the new yarn in the last shed. Break off the yarn rather than cutting, as breaking the weft leaves a tapered end and the join will show up less. I try to make the join near the selvedge as it seems to show up less than if it is in the centre.

Weave a few centimetres (inches) until you get used to the movements, then put another colour onto another shuttle and weave stripes. To join in another colour, overlap the colours as in photo 3.7. Don't leave ends hanging out the side. They will only need darning in when the weaving is off the loom and this is very time consuming. If you are changing colours every 2 picks, the colours can be carried up the selvedge (photo 3.8, page 84), but for longer stripes, break off and rejoin the yarn.

As the woven cloth is wound onto the cloth beam, the knots at the beginning of the warp may push through and leave bumps. A stick or slat placed across will cover the knots.

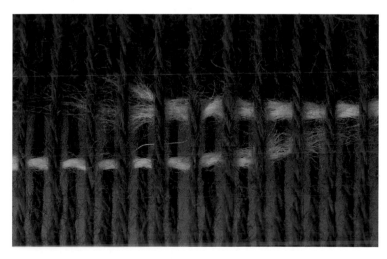

3.7 Overlapping join

Threading draft

Woven cloth

Lift plan

Figure 3.CT Plain weave draft for table looms

WEAVING DRAFTS

The previous instructions for plain weave have been written in words. This gets very long-winded, especially when the weaving project gets more complex. Weaving drafts are a type of weaving shorthand which makes writing instructions much quicker. When I first started weaving I found these drafts confusing, and many weaving books write them out in different ways (Appendix D, pages 182–83, for examples). But it makes sense to understand these drafts from the beginning, before they get too complicated.

Originally I used graph paper to write out my drafts, and many weavers still do this. Now I use computer software written especially for weaving and this is much quicker. The drafts in this book have been done on Weavepoint 7, from AVL. See Appendix D, pages 182–83, for more details on using computer software for drafts.

The threading part of the draft is written in the top left quadrant and is the same for both floor and table looms. You begin threading from the right to the left, starting with the first warp end through the heddle eye on shaft 1, followed by 2, 3, 4, then back to 1 again. This is the same as the graph in figure 2.E, page 51, in the previous chapter.

It is the weaving sequence that is written differently for floor and table looms, so from now on I will give two separate drafts for each structure. Just read the correct one for your loom.

Table looms: On these looms, each shaft is lifted independently. The instructions are written in the lower right quadrant of the draft. These are read from top to bottom, so you can see that the first lift is for shafts 1 &

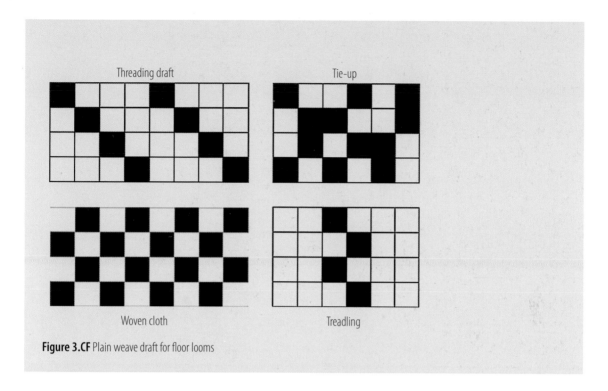

Threading draft

Tie-up

Woven cloth

Treadling

Figure 3.CF Plain weave draft for floor looms

3 to rise. This quadrant of the draft is sometimes called the 'lift plan'.
Floor looms: Here the shafts are lifted by depressing the treadles,
and one or more shafts can be lifted by one treadle, depending on
which shaft is tied to which treadle. The tie-up is shown in the upper
right quadrant (figure 2.G, page 55). Here we have the plain weave
shafts tied to the centre two treadles, which are tied to shafts 1 & 3, 2
& 4. The treadling draft is in the lower right-hand quadrant and is also
read from top to bottom.

Look at the first square in the top of the treadling draft. Follow it
up to the tie-up quadrant, and you can see that this treadle is tied to
shafts 1 & 3. Follow the second pick up and this means you lift 2 & 4.
You will soon get to the stage where one glance at the treadling draft
will tell you which treadle to depress. It is like reading music, a symbol
like a square is easier to recognise than a number.
Direct tie-up: Some floor looms have what is called a 'direct tie-up'
where each treadle is tied directly (without lamms) to a single shaft.
For these looms, follow the table loom drafts. When you need to
raise two shafts at once, use two feet. To lift three shafts depress one
treadle with one foot and the other two treadles with the other foot.
It helps to have big feet!

The lower left quadrant on both table and floor loom drafts is a
graphic description of what the cloth looks like on the loom. A black
square is a warp end on the cloth surface, a white square is a weft
thread on the surface. This quadrant is called the draw-down. Don't
worry about understanding the draw-down at this stage.

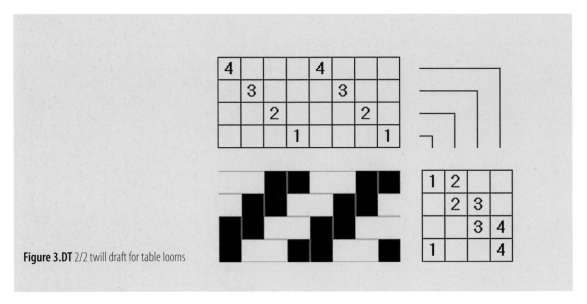

Figure 3.DT 2/2 twill draft for table looms

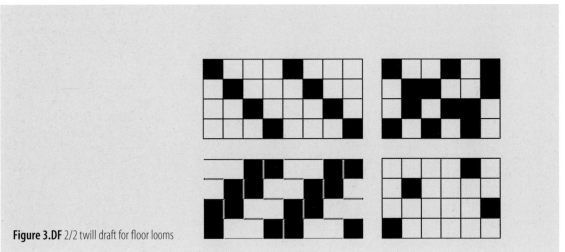

Figure 3.DF 2/2 twill draft for floor looms

2/2 TWILL

Another common weave is a 2/2 twill (figure 2.B, page 38). This weave structure makes a thicker, more flexible cloth. It pulls in more at the sides because, as each end goes over and under two warp ends, not one as in plain weave, the weft packs down more. This is the reason that it is not usual to weave both these structures in one piece of cloth, but as this is just a practice piece, it doesn't matter at this stage. Normally twill weaves have the warp sett closer than with plain weave because twill has less intersections, but I don't want to confuse you more than you are already so we can use the same sett of 8 e.p.2.5cm (1in).

You will notice that the threading is the same as for plain weave; it is just the weaving sequence that has changed. There are 4 picks to a repeat. With a table loom weave the following sequence:

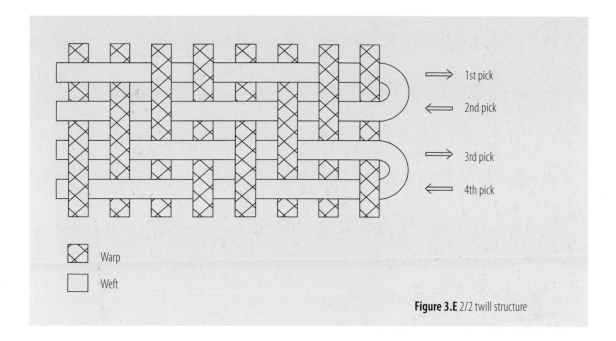

⟹ 1st pick

⟸ 2nd pick

⟹ 3rd pick

⟸ 4th pick

⊠ Warp

☐ Weft

Figure 3.E 2/2 twill structure

First pick has shafts 1 & 2 raised.
Second pick 2 & 3.
Third pick 3 & 4.
Fourth pick 4 & 1. Then begin at the beginning again.
If you are using a floor loom, depress the treadles in the order shown in figure 3.DF. This is 'walking the treadles' as described on page 55. Read the treadling draft from the top down. To see which treadles to depress, follow the first black square up to the tie-down and you will see that you lift shafts 1 & 2 for the first pick, and so on, the same as the table loom sequence.

Do not beat as hard as you did for the plain weave. To test the beating, look at the angle of the twill line. It should be at 45 degrees.

Missed selvedge ends

With 2/2 twill you may find that an outside warp end is missed out. When I first began weaving, I just picked up this missed end with my shuttle. Then I was told a very simple trick. Just change the side you throw the shuttle from. Break off the weft, tuck the end in and throw from the opposite side. You only have to do this once.

You can work this sequence out before you begin weaving, but changing sides is a good trick to remember and is what I usually do. However, if you are mathematically inclined this is what to do. If you began your threading on shaft 1 (an odd-numbered shaft) and finished on shaft 4 (an even-numbered shaft), start the sequence of lifting 1 & 2 with the shuttle entering on the even side. Some weave patterns need a special threading to make a good selvedge, but this will be pointed out in the instructions for that pattern.

3.8 Shuttle order when using two shuttles

Weaving 2/2 twill using two shuttles

Weave a few centimetres (inches) in the twill sequence, again changing colours every now and then. Then try using both shuttles at once changing colours every 2 picks.

This will get you used to weaving with two shuttles when carrying the weft up the sides and give you practice in making neat selvedges. Use the shuttles in the same order; that is, pass one shuttle through and place it on the weaving in front of you. Pass the next shuttle through in the same direction, and place it behind the first shuttle and nearer to you. Keep doing this; the last shuttle used always gets placed behind the other shuttle.

ADVANCING THE WARP

This is best done frequently as you weave because the beater is most efficient when it hits the fell of the cloth at right angles. How often you wind on will depend on how much room you have between the front beam and the shafts but every 5–8cm (2–3in) is a good guide. How you wind on will depend on how your loom works. Make sure the warp tension is the same after advancing the warp so check by running the back of your hand over it.

RATCHET AND PAWL SYSTEM

Loosen the warp beam by lifting the pawl out of the ratchet teeth on the warp beam. This can be done by hand at the back of the loom or by a lever at the front of the loom. Do not let too much warp unwind. Then, without lifting the front pawl, advance the warp by turning the cloth beam ratchet.

FRICTION BRAKE

This is mainly found on floor looms (photo 2.23, page 48). A metal cylinder on one end of the warp beam has a wire cable wrapped around it two or three times, without overlapping, and the other end of the cable is attached to a lever, which can be operated at the front of the loom. When the cable tension is released, the warp beam can be unwound and the warp is advanced.

CORRECTING ERRORS

Many of these are easier done while the warp is under tension on the loom.

Skipped warp ends

These are caused by your shuttle not passing cleanly through the shed and picking up a few upper or lower warp ends. Hopefully you will notice this when you have just finished that pick, in which case it is simple to just undo this last pick. If you notice a skipped end and you are a few centimetres (inches) past, mark it with a coloured tag of yarn and mend it when the weaving is off the loom.

Broken warp ends

These happen to the best of weavers. If the selvedge ends keep breaking, check that the sides have not pulled in too much. Bring the beater up to the fell and see if the warp selvedge ends run almost in a straight line from the reed to the cloth. If the selvedge ends pull in too much, the strain will cause the ends to continually break. Sometimes it is best to undo the weaving until you reach a point where the selvedges are straight and then re-weave.

To replace a broken end, break off a matching piece of the warp yarn long enough to stretch from the fell of the cloth to about a metre (yard) over the back beam. Take this thread through the heddle and reed in the same position as the broken end and attach one end of it to the fell of the cloth where the broken end emerged. Put a pin in the cloth at this point and take the replacement thread around the pin in a figure of eight a couple of times.

Go to the back of the loom, remove the broken end and let it hang over the back beam. Weigh the replacement thread with something so it is the same tension as the rest of the warp. Film cannisters filled with the right number of coins were very useful as the lid could be used to hold the yarn, but in this digital age these are hard to find. I have some large bulldog clips which do the trick.

When the broken end can be brought forward and reaches past the fell of the cloth, re-thread it in the correct heddle and reed dent and again pin it into the cloth. Remove the replacement thread. The beginning and end of the threads will need to be darned in when the cloth is taken off the loom and before it is washed. I usually remove the pins when the woven cloth reaches the cloth beam, otherwise they can catch on the next layer of cloth.

3.9 Attaching the replacement end on the woven cloth at the fell

3.10 Weighting the replacement end at the back of the loom

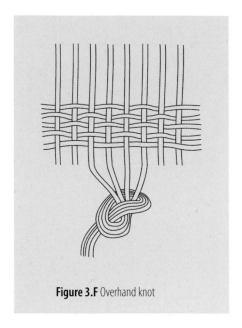

Figure 3.F Overhand knot

If there are knots in the warp yarn and these won't go through the dents in the reed, treat these as broken threads. If the knot will pass through but is noticeable, put a marker tie in and, when the cloth is removed from the loom, cut out the knot and darn in a new replacement thread.

Weave until you feel your selvedges are reasonably tidy, then get ready to weave the scarf. Tuck in the last weft pick and break it off. Change sheds and place a ruler across the shed in shafts 1 & 3. Change to shafts 2 & 4 and place another ruler across. It is easier to remove two rulers than one. Move these rulers up to leave a gap of about 15cm (6in) between the sampler you have just finished and the scarf. As we are going to knot the ends of the scarf, we will need a reasonable length for the fringe. Remove these sticks when you have woven about 2.5cm (1in).

▪ WEAVING THE SCARF

Weave the scarf in either plain weave or twill. If you weave it in twill the scarf will be somewhat thicker, softer and narrower than one woven in plain weave. Because you are weaving a lightweight scarf, beat gently, and, if you are weaving the 2/2 twill, check the 45-degree angle. Place measuring markers every 15cm (6in) as it is not a good idea to unwind the woven cloth to see how far you have woven as this makes the tension uneven. I use ties in a contrasting yarn knotted into the selvedge ends as markers. For contrast, a few picks of a contrasting yarn of the same thickness can be woven as a stripe at both ends of the scarf.

When the scarf is 1.8m (6ft) long, turn in and break off the weft after the last weft pick. Advance the warp so there is 15cm (6in) past the weaving, then cut the scarf off the loom. This 15cm (6in) will be the end fringe. Loosen the scarf at the front ratchet, and unwind it back to the beginning.

It is easier to cut out the heading yarn while the weaving is still on the loom. Cut through the little loops at each selvedge and pull out the heading yarn. Then loosen the triple knots by pulling on one of the tails and undo the knots. Now you can admire your weaving, although it will not look its best until it is washed.

Lay the length on a table and cut through the warp dividing the sampler and the scarf, leaving about 15cm (6in) on the scarf end for the knotted fringe. Knot the scarf ends as soon as possible as weaving comes undone very easily before it is washed. Use an overhand knot for both ends. Take 4 ends, make the overhand knot and slip it up until it meets the woven edge.

The ends could also be hemstitched (figures 4.A, 4.B and 4.C, page 95). Trim both ends to the same length. The sampler can be knotted at both ends in the same manner.

3.11 Finished scarf

3.12 Scarf detail

CHECK FOR MISTAKES

Mending should be done before the scarf is washed, as after washing the warp and weft will merge and the mend is less noticeable.

Where the warp ends were broken, needle weave the tails in with a darning needle for about 2.5cm (1in) each end of the replacement end, then trim.

Check for any skipped warp or weft ends. Mend these by taking a short length of the matching yarn and a darning needle and, following the correct sequence, needle weave this thread over and under the warp/weft threads for about 2.5cm (1in) each side of the skip. Leave tails of about 3–5cm (1–2in). Trim these ends, then cut out the skipped yarn.

Check to see if your beating was even. Hold the scarf up to the light to see any areas where the beating was closer or further apart than the rest of the weaving. As this is your first woven article, it would be a miracle if you didn't have some discrepancies. Washing will certainly help but it is a good idea just to check it anyway, even if you can't do much about it at this stage.

WASHING

Most weaving is not considered finished until it is washed. This blends the warp and weft together and makes the weaving look like a piece of fabric, not just threads crossed over each other. There are many ways of washing fabric, depending on the yarn and the use of the finished article. Other methods will be covered in subsequent chapters.

For this project, lay the scarf in a bath of warm, soapy water. Knead it slightly, then rinse it in warm water and squeeze out the excess water. You can roll the scarf in a towel, then stand on the towel to do this. Do not wring it as this can leave creases. Lay it flat to dry, then press while slightly damp. Wash the sampler in the same way. When dry the scarf measures 175cm (69in) x 23cm (9in). On the loom it measures 182cm (71½in) x 25cm (10in). The contraction is caused partly by the yarn shrinking when washed and partly because the weaving is under tension on the loom and relaxes when it is removed. So if you want to be exact in your measurements, always allow for this contraction in your warp plan.

Now you can gloat over your weaving and wear it with pride. See the difference between the selvedges from the start of your weaving to the end. It is amazing how quickly they improve.

Reflections

This book gives you step-by-step directions on how to weave specific projects. This is how most of us start, with or without a teacher to guide us. But these projects are just a starting point.

Tien Chiu, a very experienced weaver, gave me some thoughts I would like to share with you. There comes a time when you want to design your own projects and a good way to begin this thought process is to ask yourself the following questions at the end of every project.

- Did I enjoy this project?
- What parts did I enjoy the most?
- What parts did I not enjoy doing?
- What did I learn?
- What can I improve about the finished project?

By reflecting on these questions, you will gradually have the confidence to branch out and become bolder in the planning and designing of your own work.

Part II

PROJECTS

4.1 Three runners

Table runners

You will learn how to weave stripes, twill and plain weave

Minimum loom width: 45cm (18in)

For your second warp, table runners are quick to weave and fun to do, especially if you choose your favourite colours.

Runners should be:

- easy wash and colour fast
- hard-wearing
- stable

4.2 Twill runner

CHARACTERISTICS

Easy wash and colour fast: Table runners will be washed often. I have woven wool table runners, but I find cotton or cottolin (a mixture of linen and cotton) the best to use. The linen adds a crisp feel to the yarn. Both these yarns can withstand many washes and won't shrink or lose colour in the process. Linen is also a suitable yarn for table runners, but is best left until you have more experience. Linen yarns do not shrink so a linen cotton mix won't shrink as much as a pure cotton yarn.

Cotton and cottolin yarns are easy to obtain and have a wide colour range. The cottolin I have chosen for this project is 60% cotton, 40% linen. As much of the cottolin comes from Scandinavia, it is useful to know that cotton is 'bomull' in Swedish and linen is 'lin'.

Hard-wearing: Cotton and cotton-blend yarns seem to be more water resistant than most wools, so spills are not absorbed easily.

Stable: Runners must be firm enough so they will not slide or move about on a slippery surface like a table.

Size: Runners can be any size, and woven to fit any surface. I prefer rectangular runners, as we have a rectangular table, but they can be any shape.

4.1 Three runners
A Plain weave stripes
B 2/2 twill
C Plain weave plaid

WARP PLAN

Warp yarn: 22/2 cottolin, 6590m/kg (3270yd/lb). This is about equivalent to an 8/2 cotton.

4 colours: #2028 dark blue, #2035 light green, #2038 dark green, #2074 medium blue. 250gm (9oz) in each cone

Wraps: 34 per 2.5cm (1in)

Weft yarn: Same as warp

Warp length: 3 runners 66cm (26in) each
+ 48cm (19in) for fringes = 246cm (97in)
Wastage = 91cm (36in)
Sampling = 76cm (30in)
Total warp (rounded up) = 4.5m (15ft)

Width in reed: 48cm (19in) 380 ends

Sett: Warp — 20 e.p.2.5cm (1in)
Weft — 20 p.p.2.5cm (1in)

Reed: 10-dent

Woven length on loom: Each runner 66cm (26in)

Threading: Straight draw 1, 2, 3, 4

Structure: Plain weave and 2/2 twill

Finished size after washing: Each runner, excluding fringes:
43cm (17in) wide by 60cm (23½in) long

Finishing: Hemstitching

Weight of one finished runner: 85gm (3oz)

Winding the warp: See the instructions in Chapter 2, photos 2.4–2.10, pages 39–52. I wound two warps, with 24cm (9½in) of width in each half. This is the best way to wind wider warps as otherwise the pegs on the warping board can start to angle in under the warp tension and the outside ends become shorter than the inside ends. Wind the first warp, put in all the correct ties, remove it from the warping board and put it in a safe place. Then wind the second warp. Each warp is 4.5m (15ft) long.

Place the four cones of yarn on the floor, and keep them in the same order as you wind. When I had wound the first dark blue stripe, I placed that cone at the back of the colour order and so on. The width of the stripes was random, although I kept to the same sequence of dark blue, dark green, medium blue, light green. No stripe was more than 5cm (2in) wide, and none were under 1cm (½in). Setting some parameters such as this makes it easy to choose the colours as it is difficult to be completely random. Tie each group of 20 ends with a counting tie as you go.

Threading: Push 48 heddles to the centre of the loom, and thread with a straight draw on four shafts: 1, 2, 3, 4 (figures 3.CT, page 80 and 3.CF, page 81). Remember to check as you go and tie each group of 20 in a slip knot. You should have 19 slip knots when you have finished and end up with the last thread on shaft 4.

Sleying: The best reed to use is a 10-dent reed. If you have other sizes, see Appendix A, page 175. Place 2 ends in each dent.

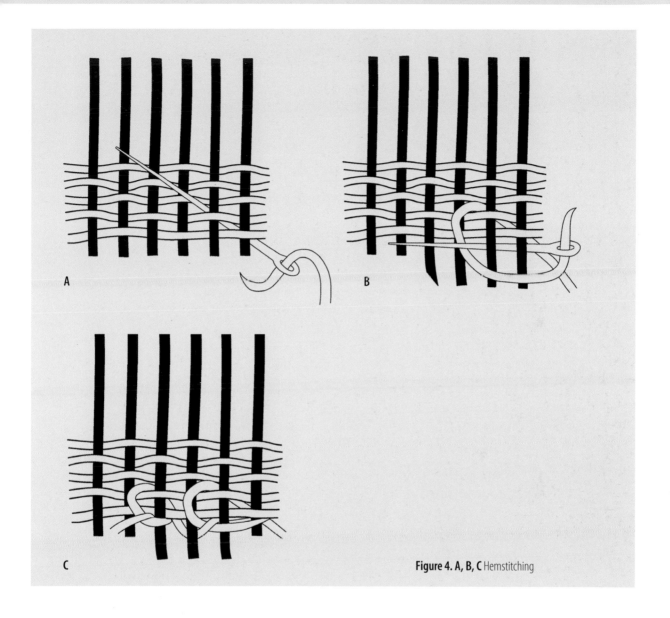

Figure 4. A, B, C Hemstitching

Weaving: Weave a heading, then try some of the four colours as the weft to see which you prefer. As the warp has brightly coloured stripes, choosing one of the four colours as the weft will emphasise the warp stripes.

Hemstitching: On this sample we will practise hemstitching. I seemed to have a mental block about this finishing stitch, and had to be shown several times. But it is such a strong, neat finish that it is worth persevering with. Leave a tail of the weft yarn hanging out of the right selvedge (if you are right-handed; out the left side if you are left-handed) about three times the width of the cloth on the loom and use this tail for the stitching. For the size of this cottolin, I hemstitched in groups of four. With finer threads I may group the stitches in sixes; for thicker threads I may hemstitch in twos.

4.3 Twill and plain weave

If you find the background distracting as you hemstitch, place a piece of white or black cloth or paper behind the warp threads.

Here are some of the things you can sample:

- Plain weave, lifting 1 & 3, 2 & 4 alternately in one of the colours.
- Plaids, using all four of the colours, either in random weft stripes or with all the stripes the same width.
- 2/2 twill, either in one of the colours or in the plaid sequence (figures 3.DT and 3.DF, page 82, for the weaving draft).

Do not mix plain weave and twill in the same runner as twill pulls in more than plain weave (photo 4.4) because it crosses over 2 ends at a time, whereas plain weave crosses over one. If you do interchange twill and plain weave frequently, you will get uneven selvedges (as you can see here in the sample).

When you are changing colours in the weft stripes, break off the old yarn about 5cm (2in) out from the selvedge of the last pick and tuck the end into the next shed. With the new colour, overlap the new end over the tucked-in end by about 3cm (1in) in the same shed. I try to do this on alternate sides so I am not always making the join on the same side.

See figures 3.CT, page 80 and 3.CF, page 81, for the plain weave draft; and figures 3.DT and 3.DF, page 82, for the twill draft.

If you find you are missing the outside selvedge end when weaving 2/2 twill, see page 83 to correct this. I find it helps to repeat the sequence to myself as I weave, and remember which side the shuttle comes from for each pick. If the correct sequence is that I lift shafts 1 & 2 from the right, I know I have made a mistake if I find I am weaving this pick from the left. It is tedious to unpick several centimetres (inches) of weaving because you have got one pick wrong. Beat with a reasonably firm beat, about 20 picks to 2.5cm (1in).

When you have finished sampling, hemstitch the other end and leave a gap for the fringes of about 15cm (6in).

4.4 Sample

Decide which of the colours and structures on your sampler you prefer and weave the first runner 66cm (26in) long. Remember to hemstitch both ends. It is very difficult to hemstitch once the cloth has been cut from the loom. I know this as it has happened to me several times and I didn't enjoy the experience.

When you have finished that runner, hemstitch the end, leave a space of 15cm (6in) in between and weave the second and third runners in another colour or pattern. When you have finished the last runner, leave a fringe of 8cm (3in) and cut the warp from the loom. Cut the runners and sample apart, leaving an 8cm (3in) fringe on each end.

Check for any mistakes and mend these, then put the runners in the washing machine. I usually use a warm wash cycle. Lay the runners flat to dry. When they are nearly dry, press them with a steam iron. You will notice the difference between the twill runner (if you have woven one in the 2/2 twill), as it will be more flexible and slightly narrower than the plain weave runners.

There will also be quite a bit of shrinkage in both the width and length (5cm (2in)). I am tough when I wash woven articles that have to be washed often, which is why I washed these in the washing machine. When I first began weaving I was so gentle and carefully hand washed everything. Now, especially for articles I sell, I give them a thorough wash, as this is how they will be handled after they are sold or given away.

Ask yourself:

- Did I enjoy this project?
- What parts did I enjoy the most?
- What parts did I not enjoy doing?
- What did I learn?
- What can I improve about the finished project?

97

5.1 Wrap

Mohair wrap

You will learn how to weave with sticky yarns

Minimum loom width: 50cm (20in)

For your third project, a mohair wrap is an easy and fun garment to weave. Because mohair is such a textured yarn, no pattern is needed and the yarn adds all the surface interest you will need. With thick yarn, it is quick to warp and thread the loom, and the weaving is also fast. A wrap is really just like a big scarf.

I have made wraps from a large square piece of fabric, folded into a triangle shape, but this requires a large loom of at least 1.20m (4ft) wide. This type of wrap is more commonly called a shawl. Wraps should be:

- warm
- soft next to the skin
- rectangular in size
- decorative
- flexible

CHARACTERISTICS

Warmth: I have chosen looped mohair for this wrap because it is such a warm, inviting yarn. The loops trap air and will keep the wearer warm, even though the threads are not placed close together. Mohair also has good insulating qualities.

Soft: Mohair is a very soft and springy yarn, and most people will find it feels good next to the skin.

Size: I make my wraps large, both in width and in length, as I like to be able to wrap them right around my shoulders or throw one end over one shoulder. A finished size of about 50cm (20in) wide and 2.5m (8ft) long, including the fringe, is a good size.

Decorative: Because the yarn has such an interesting texture, any pattern is lost in the finished cloth so plain weave is all that is needed.

Flexible: Wraps need to be able to drape easily around the body, so the sett and beat are open.

YARN

Mohair comes from the fibre of the Angora goat, has a high lustre and is very strong. It is very soft, and feels good next to your skin. Personally I prefer to wear looped mohair rather than brushed mohair, which is brushed to break up the loops. This process gives it a fuzzy surface which can be irritating. When choosing the yarn, rub a little under your chin to see how it feels.

Look at the label before you buy. Most mohair yarns are mixed with a varying proportion of wool and/or nylon. A blend of about 80–90% mohair has a high proportion of mohair and a luxurious feel. Watch out, however, for acrylic yarns that are called mohair; they don't have the qualities of real mohair. Because mohair has a high lustre and takes dyes well, colours are usually strong and bright.

WARP PLAN
Warp yarn: Mohair, 2015m/kg (1000yd/lb)
Wraps: 12 per 2.5cm (1in)
Weft yarn: Same as warp
Warp length: 1 wrap 2.3m (7½ft)
   + 15cm (6in) for fringes = 2.5m (8ft)
   Wastage = 91cm (36in)
   Total warp (rounded up) = 3.5m (11½ft)
Weight of warp and weft yarn required: Blue = 350gm (12½oz)
   Grey = 50gm (2oz)
   Black = 10gm (½oz)
Width in reed: 50cm (20in) 120 ends
Sett: Warp — 6 e.p.2.5cm (1in)
   Weft — 6 p.p.2.5cm (1in)
Reed: 6 or 12
Woven length on loom: 2.3m (7½ft)
Threading: Straight draw 1, 2, 3, 4
Structure: Plain weave
Finished size after washing: 48cm (19in) wide by 2.3m (7½ft) long,
   excluding fringes
Finishing: Knotted fringe
Weight of finished wrap: 320gm (11½oz)
Winding the warp: Because mohair is very sticky, you will need to wind the warp with crosses at both ends, following the instruction on page 62. Sticky warps like this will not slide over the cross sticks, and it is a real tussle to unstick the ends.

Wind a warp 3.5m (11½ft) long and 50cm (20in) wide. The colour sequence is as follows: 24 ends blue, 1 black, 16 grey, 1 black, 30 blue, 1 black, 10 grey, 1 black, 36 blue.

It will help to wind the correct number in each colour if you cross off each colour change as you wind. Notice that the warp stripes are asymmetrical. Outlining each grey strip with one end of black gives a better definition to the stripes.

If you are using a warping board, it will be easier if you wind the warp in two sections, with 25cm (10in) in each section. Because this is a thick warp yarn, it will build up quickly on the pegs and if you wind the complete warp at once, the threads tend to slip off the pegs. Also the pegs tend to bend inwards under the weight, meaning the last threads will be shorter than the first ones. So wind half, make all the usual ties around the cross etc. as normal, then remove it from the board. Then wind the other half. Check when you put the warps on the back rod that the colour order is still correct. With a warping mill, also wind in two sections.

Tie each group of 6 ends in the counting tie (20 ties). When joining the colours, do so at either peg A or peg D (photo 2.4, page 39) with an overhand knot. Wind the warp onto the warp beam as per the instructions on page 46, if you have a helper, or page 65 if you are beginning on your own.

Threading: This draft, threading the warp ends on shafts 1, 2, 3, 4, then repeating this sequence, is called a straight draw. Usually it is not necessary to write out this simple threading as a draft first. From the right side of the shafts, push 15 heddles across to the centre on each shaft. Thread the first 8 ends, check, then tie with a slip knot. When you get to the centre, just push across the heddles as you need them. There is no need to count out the heddles on the left of the centre line. As there are 120 ends, you should end up with the last end on the left on shaft 4, and 15 slip knots.

Sleying: Put the reed back in the beater if you have removed it. If you have a 6-dent reed, place 1 end in each dent. If you have a 12-dent reed, place 1 end in every second dent. For other reeds, see the table in Appendix A, page 175.

Weaving: Weave a heading as described on page 56. Wind the blue weft yarn onto a shuttle. As this weft yarn is thick, a stick or ski shuttle will be better than the boat or end delivery shuttles which are best suited to finer yarns. As you will be knotting the ends, you can start weaving the wrap straight after weaving the heading; there is no need to place a dividing stick across.

With the blue weft, and beating gently to give 6 weft picks to 2.5cm (1in), weave for 2.3m (7½ft). Remember to mark every 30cm (12in) or so to measure how far you have woven. Follow drafts in figures 3.CT, page 80 and 3.CF, page 81, in Chapter 3.

As this yarn is sticky, change sheds just as the beater hits the last weft pick if you are using a floor loom. If you do this, the returning beater will clear the shed. If the shed still doesn't clear, give the beater a few waggles back and forth after you have beaten the last pick. If you are using a table loom, you can change into the next shed, then beat, as this also clears the shed.

If you wish, you can replicate one or both of the warp stripes in the black and grey across both ends of the wrap, about 10cm (4in) from each end. When you reach 2.3m (7½ft), cut the warp off, leaving 8cm (3in) for the fringe.

Finishing and washing: Knot both ends immediately with an overhand knot, as on page 86, as this loose weaving will come undone quickly, then wash in warm soapy water, rinse and dry lying flat. Do not press.

Ask yourself:

- Did I enjoy this project?
- What parts did I enjoy the most?
- What parts did I not enjoy doing?
- What did I learn?
- What can I improve about the finished project?

6.1 Dish towels

Dish towels

You will learn how to thread a small block pattern

Minimum loom width: 61cm (24in)

I think every weaver has woven a dish towel (in New Zealand we call them tea towels) in their weaving life. I have a collection of dish towels that I have been given by weaving friends over the years. I felt they were too attractive to use, so I kept them in a cupboard until one day I realised how silly this was. Now I use them all the time and think about the weavers who lovingly wove them for me.

Dish towels should be:

- absorbent
- hard-wearing
- rectangular in size
- machine washable
- should not need ironing
- colour fast

CHARACTERISTICS

Absorbent: Cotton or cottolin, a mixture of cotton and linen, is best. The absorbency is mainly determined by the amount of twist. A low-twist cotton is softer and more absorbent than high-twist cotton. There are two types of cotton: mercerised (also called pearl/pearle cotton) and unmercerised. The mercerising process alters the chemical structure of the cotton, adding lustre, strength and a greater affinity to dye. There is probably a better range of brighter colours with mercerised cotton. I once had some expensive linen dish towels and they lasted forever but it took many washes before they became soft and absorbent.

Hard-wearing: Dish towels are washed often, so need to stand up to frequent washing in the washing machine. Cotton and cottolin both meet this requirement. Cottolin, by the addition of linen, is more hard-wearing than plain cotton. This frequent washing makes fringes undesirable, and the strongest finish is to machine hem the ends.

Size: I like reasonably large towels so a finished size of 43cm (17in) x 71cm (28in) is what you will aim for. Because this is rather a large expanse of cloth, you will add stripes in both the warp and weft to add interest.

Colour fast: Because dish towels need frequent machine washing, the yarn must be colour fast. If in doubt, test for this first. Put some of the coloured yarn in boiling water with detergent and leave for a day or two. You can also test for colour fastness by putting some of the yarn

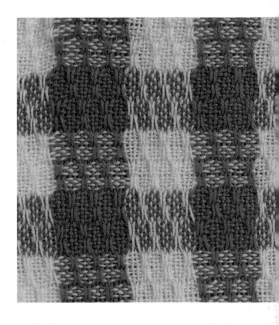

6.2 Detail

103

in a matchbox, and exposing half to the sun. Compare the two halves.
Non-iron: A textured surface needs little or no ironing, compared to a plain flat surface. Nowadays there are probably not many people left like my mother, who always ironed her tea towels! There are many textured structures which will be suitable: Ms and Os, which I have chosen, is one of the best, but basket weave, waffle weave, Swedish lace and huckaback are also good choices. Because the texture comes from the weave structure, the yarn chosen is plain, without slubs.

YARN

I have chosen a soft white 8/2 mercerised cotton for the main body of these towels. One of the best things about cotton yarn is that it is readily available in a wide range of colours. The pink stripes are also an 8/2 mercerised cotton. It is not a good idea to mix different types of yarns in one fabric because the shrinkage may be different. For slightly thicker towels, you could use a 6/2 with the same sett.

WARP PLAN

Warp yarn: 8/2 white and pink mercerised cotton, 6770m/kg (3360yd/lb)

Wraps: 32 per 2.5cm (1in)

Weft: Same as warp

Warp length: 2 towels 81cm (32in) each = 162cm (64in)
Wastage = 91cm (36in)
Total warp (rounded up) = 3m (10ft)

Weight of warp and weft yarn required: White = 220gm (8oz)
Pink = 55gm (2oz)

Width in reed: 51cm (20in) 328 ends. I have added an extra 8 selvedge ends to strengthen the selvedge; 4 each side.

Sett: Warp — 16 e.p.2.5cm (1in)
Weft — 16 p.p.2.5cm (1in)

Reed: 8-dent

Woven length on loom: Each towel 81cm (32in). This allows for a 2.5cm (1in) hem on each end.

Threading: Ms and Os

Finished size after washing: 69cm (27in) x 43cm (17in) after hemming

Finishing: Machine hemmed

Weight of one towel: 95gm (3½oz)

Winding the warp: Wind a warp 3m (10ft) long, and 51cm (20in) wide. Tie the 4 selvedge ends in one counting tie, then each 2.5cm (1in) — 16 ends — with counting ties; 22 in all. As you will be adding stripes, the colour sequence is as follows: 36 ends white, 16 ends pink, 16 ends white, 16 ends pink, 160 ends white, 16 ends pink, 16 ends white, 16 ends pink, 36 ends white, to give a total of 328. To save confusion, write this colour sequence on a sheet of paper and, as you wind each block of colour, cross it off. When changing to a different colour, join it with an overhand knot (page 86) at peg A.

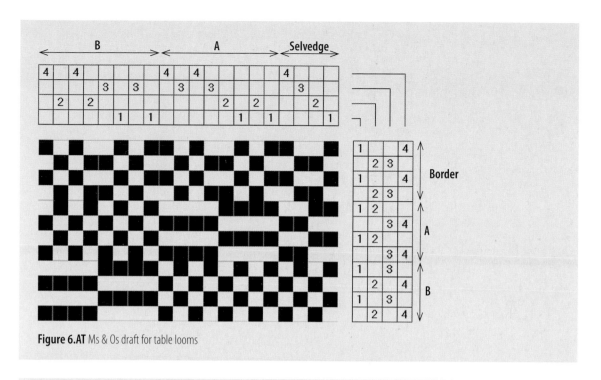

Figure 6.AT Ms & Os draft for table looms

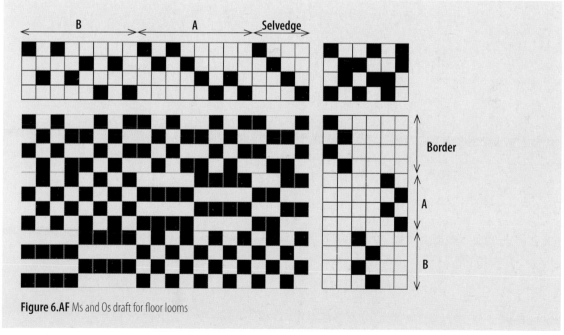

Figure 6.AF Ms and Os draft for floor looms

Because there are 8 ends in each block of the pattern draft, the total number of ends, excluding the selvedge ends, must be divisible by 8.

As there are 328 ends in this warp, try winding from two cones or balls of the one colour at once, as on page 62. This is twice as quick as winding separate threads.

Wind the warp onto the warp beam as per the instructions on page 46 if you have a helper, or page 65 if you are beaming on your own.

Threading: Follow the drafts in figures 6.AT and 6.AF, page 105, for the threading. You will see the threading of 1, 2, 3, 4 at both ends to strengthen the selvedges.

In this weave structure, there are two blocks in the threading, A and B (8 ends in each block), and two blocks in the treadling, A and B (4 picks in each block). One block will weave plain weave while the other block weaves the pattern of **floats**. Then the blocks exchange places.

If you look at the draw-down (the lower left quandrant), you will see why I have added an extra 8 ends, 4 each side, as this leaves a strong border, with less floats, at each selvedge.

From the right side of the shaft, push across 41 heddles on each of the four shafts to the centre. Begin threading the heddles from the right side of this group. Start from the right side of the draft and move to the left. When you have threaded the first 4 selvedge ends, check, then tie a slip knot (page 49) with these 4 ends. Then thread each block of eight, A and B, repeating them alternately, check, then tie a slip knot in each block until you reach the last 4 ends at the left selvedge (threading 1, 2, 3, 4 again). Check, then tie these four selvedge ends in a slip knot. There should be 42 slip knots when you have finished.

If you finish the threading with ends missing or left over, you have either counted the warp incorrectly or made a mistake in the threading. Checking then tying each block means you should pick up mistakes as you go.

Sleying: If possible use an 8-dent reed and place 2 ends in each dent. If you have a 10-dent reed, sett at 15 e.p.2.5cm (1in) (2/1/2/1/2/1/2/1/2/1). One end less will make very little difference. If you have other reeds, see the reed chart in Appendix A, page 175.

Weaving: Weave a heading (page 56), lifting shafts 1 & 4, 2 & 3 alternately, as this is the closest you will get to plain weave with this Ms and Os structure.

Have a play following the draft for a few centimetres (inches), repeating blocks A and B alternately, to get into the rhythm of changing the shafts and learning which shafts/treadles to use in the correct order. I find it helps if I say the shafts to be lifted to myself as I weave.

When you are ready to begin weaving the towel, place a ruler across in the next shed. Because you will be hemming the ends, a narrow border, woven in a different structure, will prevent a bulky hem. Weave for 2.5cm (1in), alternating shafts 1 & 4, then 2 & 3 at both ends of each towel in the white cotton.

Hemstitch with 4 ends in each group at the end (page 95) with the weft yarn in the white cotton.

Follow the treadling plan in drafts 6.A. The blocks alternate throughout the length. On the surface you will see weft floats, and the cloth is reversible. The texture and floats will not show up properly until the cloth is washed.

> **Floats** are threads, either in the warp or weft, which float over the cloth surface to add texture.

The weft colour sequence for the first 15cm (6in) is as follows:

5cm (2in) white
2.5cm (1in) pink
2.5cm (1in) white
2.5cm (1in) pink

Do not beat heavily. Cut off the colour in the stripes and join on the next colour as described on page 96 in Chapter 4. Don't take the colours up the selvedge from stripe to stripe as this makes an untidy edge. To check that you are weaving the blocks in the correct sequence, watch the pink warp stripes as the pattern shows up clearly here.

Measure the amount you have woven. It should be 15cm (6in), including the plain weave border. This is a good test of your beating. If it is less, you are beating too hard; if it is more, you are beating too loosely. The colour sequence should change at the end of a block, not in the middle.

If I want to be really fussy, I make the borders slightly longer because the warp is under a lot of tension on the loom, and therefore will contract more than the weft when the weaving is taken off the loom. For example, when weaving squares I weave them slightly higher in the length than in the width.

Continue in the white weft until the towel measures 51cm (20in) from the last pink stripe. Then repeat the colour sequence, reading from the bottom up. Finish with the 2.5cm (1in) for the hem, lifting shafts 1 & 4, 2 & 3.

Hemstitch across the end, place a ruler across in the next shed, change sheds and place another ruler across. Then begin the second towel, remembering to hemstitch.

Weave both towels, hemstitch, then cut the end towel off the loom, leaving a 2.5cm (1in) fringe. Unwind the towels from the front cloth beam and take out the heading picks by cutting the loops at each side, then pulling them out of the weaving. Undo the knots that attach the weaving to the front stick, and remove it from the loom. Cut the towels apart, and trim the fringes to match. Check for mistakes. It is better to fix these now and they are easier to do while the cloth is more open. Trim off any loose ends.

Finishing: Trim the fringes to within about 1cm (½in) of the hemstitching, then turn in the 2.5cm (1in) hem, pin and machine stitch with a matching thread.

Washing: Put the towels in the washing machine on the full cycle. I am tough when I wash articles like dish towels that will have a hard life. If your spin cycle leaves creases in the cloth, let the towels drip-dry, as these creases are hard to remove when the cloth is dry. I usually lie them flat on a bath towel, smooth them out and let them dry lying flat. If necessary, press the towels while they are slightly damp, but this will flatten the texture. You will notice how the structure shows up much more after washing.

Ask yourself:

- Did I enjoy this project?
- What parts did I enjoy the most?
- What parts did I not enjoy doing?
- What did I learn?
- What can I improve about the finished project?

7.1 Six table mats with rosepath borders

Table mats

You will learn how to thread and weave a pattern

Minimum loom width: 41cm (16in)

Table mats are a weaver's best friend. I spent my first year as a beginner weaver making table mats. They were the wrong size, I used the wrong materials, and I didn't finish them properly. I had no teacher and one very basic book to work on, but I did learn a lot in that year. This chapter will show you what I should have done.

Table mats should be:

- hard-wearing
- rectangular in shape
- large enough to allow room for cutlery and dishes
- able to prevent heat from hot plates damaging a table top
- should lie flat so plates, glasses and cutlery do not tip over
- decorative at the borders as this is the part that shows while you eat

CHARACTERISTICS

Hard wearing: As they will be washed many times, this dictates the materials. Either cotton, linen or a mixture of both (cottolin) are good choices. They will also need to be firm, which means a close sett and firm beating. Because they will be washed often, keep the fringes short as long fringes get very untidy with frequent washing. Hemstitching is a good finish and is better than knots, as thick knots make the surface uneven and can cause spills.

Shape: I usually make mine rectangular as this leaves room for the cutlery to be placed at the side of the dishes on the mat. However, I have seen square mats, which only hold the dishes.

Size: The size does depend on fashion. My first table mats were much smaller than the ones I weave now, as dishes seem to have got bigger. I weave for a finished width of about 30cm (12in) and a length of 43–46cm (17–18in).

Thickness: Use a medium weight yarn or two strands of a finer cotton used as one so the mats provide some protection for the table top.

Decoration: Borders at each end define the dish area, add interest and can be seen both when the table is set and also when eating. For these mats I have used a popular pattern: rosepath. For each mat I will weave a different version of the threading. Apparently there are 100 versions of this pattern, so there are plenty to choose from. I have never woven that many! You can choose one border pattern and

7.2 Single table mat

weave the same one for the six mats, or do a different one for each mat, as shown in the photos.

I have outlined each border with 2 picks of plain weave in the same colour as the pattern. This defines the borders (photo 7.3).

YARN

Cotton is a good choice for a beginner as it is easy to use, comes in a wide range of colours, is lightfast and will stand much washing. There are two different types of cotton. Mercerised cotton (sometimes called pearl or pearle cotton) has been chemically treated so it has a lustre and a greater affinity to dye. Therefore it dyes brighter colours than unmercerised cotton. Choose a cotton that is reasonably tightly twisted, as this makes it less absorbent than loosely spun cotton yarn. This is an advantage as spills are a part of eating, at least in my family. Mercerised cotton is usually stronger and, if tightly twisted, will shrink less than unmercerised cotton — about 10% is the norm. A loosely spun unmercerised cottons shrinks about 15%.

A slub yarn, one that has untwisted, bumpy areas at intervals, is not as strong as a plain yarn and will shed during washing. Also, if used as a warp end the slubs can abrade as they pass at tension through the reed and heddles. For these mats, we will use a plain mercerised cotton for the warp and weft. Because the decorative feature is the borders, a plain background will show the pattern up well.

Use the same yarn in different colours for the background and the pattern. If the pattern yarn shrinks at a different rate to the background yarn, the pattern borders will pull in at each end. I usually double the pattern yarn to make it stand out from the background.

Cottolin and linen will be discussed at the end of this project.

WARP PLAN

Warp yarn: 5/2 yellow mercerised cotton, 4231m/kg (2100yd/lb)
Wraps: 25 per 2.5cm (1in)
Weft: Background — same as warp
   Pattern — blue, same yarn as warp but doubled
Weight of warp and background weft (yellow) yarn required:
   450gm (16oz)
Weight of pattern weft (blue) yarn required: 80gm (3oz)
Warp length: 6 table mats 51cm (20in)
   + 30cm (12in) for all fringes = 336cm (132in)
   Wastage = 91cm (36in)
   Total warp (rounded up) = 5m (16½ft)
Width in reed: 33cm (13in) 208 ends
Sett: Warp — 16 e.p.2.5cm (1in)
   Weft — 16 p.p.2.5cm (1in)
Reed: 8 dent
Woven length on loom: Each mat 51cm (20in)
Threading: Rosepath pattern

7.3 Table mat pattern detail

Finished size after washing: 29cm (11½in) x 43cm (17in)
Finishing: Hemstitching
Weight of one table mat: 60gm (2oz)
Winding the warp: Wind a warp 5m (16½ft) long and 33cm (13in) wide. Tie each 2.5cm (1in) with counting ties; 13 in all (pages 39–42).
Threading: Push across 26 heddles from the right-hand side of the shafts to the centre on each of the four shafts. Wind the warp onto the back beam following the instructions on page 46 if you have a helper, or 65 if you are beaming on your own. Follow the draft in figure 7.AT, page 113, for the threading, starting from the right-hand side of the draft. I have written two repeats of the rosepath pattern. As there are 8 warp ends in each repeat, for the 208 ends, you will have 26 repeats. When threading, put the 8 ends through the correct heddles, check, then tie them together in a slip knot in front of the heddles. Do make sure to check as mistakes always, annoyingly, seem to be in the centre and you have to re-thread. You should have 26 slip knots when you have finished threading.
Sleying: For an 8-dent reed, place 2 ends in each dent. If you have other reeds, see the reed chart in Appendix A, page 175. If you have a 10-dent reed, sett at 15 ends per 2.5cm (2/1/2/1/2/1/2/1/2/1). One less warp end will not make much difference.
Weaving: Weave a heading (page 56). It pays to check the warp tension and for mistakes in the threading or sleying at this stage. Because mercerised cotton is slippery, when the tension is correct, tie a bow on top of the surgeon's knot attaching the warp to the front rod to prevent it from coming undone.

I have allowed some extra warp for practising on, so if you want to try the pattern before you begin the mat, do this now. Then place a ruler across and weave with the yellow weft yarn for 2.5cm (1in) of plain weave, following draft 7.AT if you have a table loom and 7.AF if you have a floor loom. Plain weave lift shafts 1 & 3, then 2 & 4 alternately. Beat reasonably hard with 16 p.p.2.5cm (1in).

Leave a metre (3 feet) or so of weft hanging from the end of the first pick for hemstitching. Leave the background weft on the shuttle after you have woven this plain weave border. Don't cut it off. Remove the ruler and hemstitch with the yellow background weft (page 95).

Weave 2 picks in the doubled blue yarn in plain weave. To keep the edges neat, place 1 weft pick across from right to left, leaving about a 2.5cm (1in) tail hanging out the right-hand selvedge. Change sheds, tuck in the yarn tail on the right, then return the shuttle to the right-hand side, crossing over the tail. Trim off the second pick of the blue pattern weft level with the selvedge on the right. Turning in the ends this way avoids a doubled turn in at one selvedge.

Weave 4 picks in the yellow background weft, again in plain weave, bringing it up the selvedge over the 2 blue picks. Because you are only carrying it up for 2 picks, this will not cause a problem.

Now follow the draft for the pattern you have chosen. Pattern 1 is the easiest to start with. Use the blue weft yarn, doubled. There are six different rosepath patterns, all about the same size. The blue yarn is used doubled for the pattern picks. There is a plain weave pick (tabby) woven between each pattern pick using the yellow yarn. This is not shown on the draft.

When I first started weaving and was not good at reading drafts, I used to write the pattern as follows. I can tell which books I used when I first began weaving as I used to pencil in the written numbers beside the weaving draft. Being self-taught, I found weaving drafts daunting to begin with. However, it is much quicker to weave following the drafts in figures 7.AT and 7.AF (page 114) and 7.BT and 7.BF (pages 115 and 116) than to follow written numbers. The following is pattern 1 written out in words.

> Lift 1 & 3 background, yellow
> 1 & 2 pattern, blue
> 2 & 4 background, yellow
> 2 & 3 pattern, blue
> 1 & 3 background, yellow
> 3 & 4 pattern, blue
> 2 & 4 background, yellow
> 1 & 4 pattern, blue

Repeat four times (16 pattern picks). Finish by repeating 1 & 3 in the yellow background weft and then a pattern pick in blue on shafts 1 & 2 to balance the pattern.

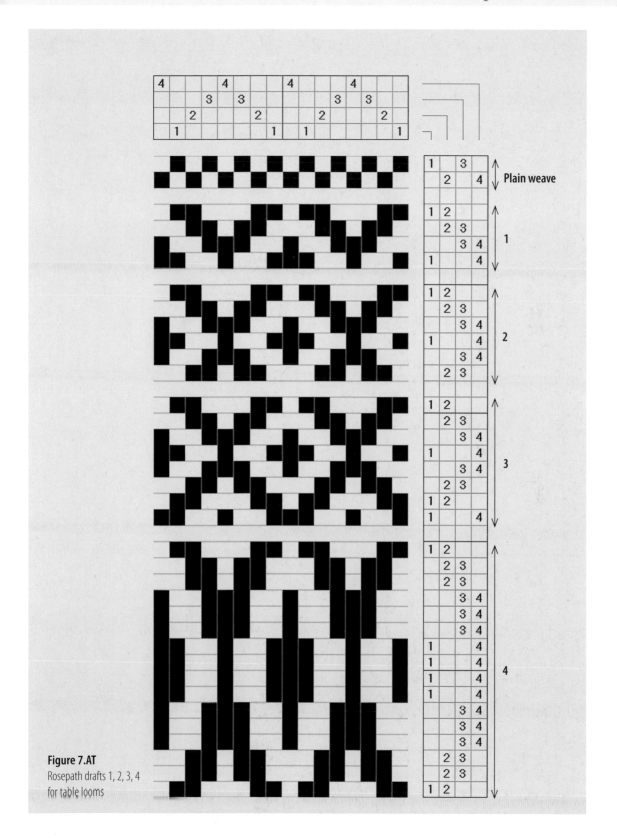

Figure 7.AT
Rosepath drafts 1, 2, 3, 4
for table looms

113

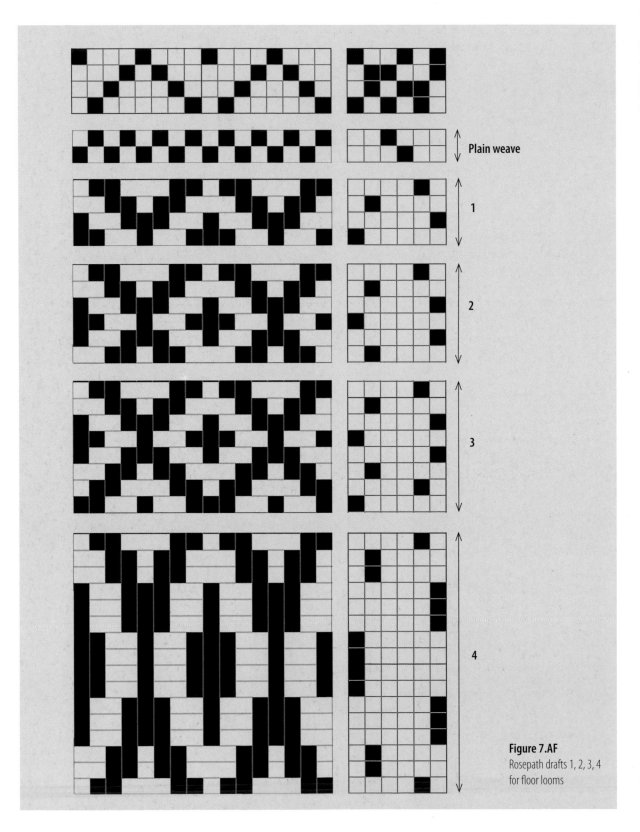

Figure 7.AF
Rosepath drafts 1, 2, 3, 4
for floor looms

Plain weave

1

2

3

4

Figure 7.BT
Rosepath drafts 5, 6
for table looms

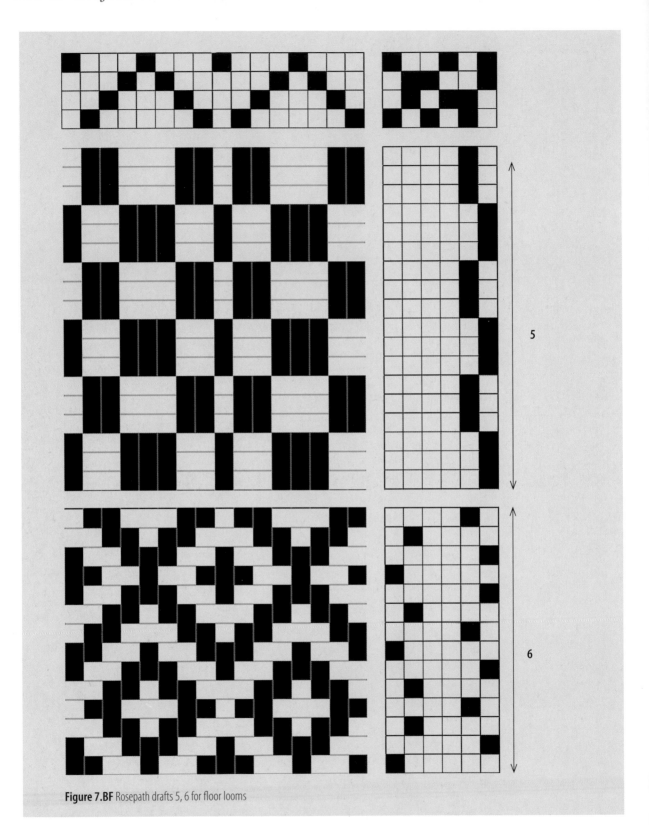

Figure 7.BF Rosepath drafts 5, 6 for floor looms

Staying on track

Because you have two shuttles working, one weaving the pattern and one the plain weave in between, it is easy to get lost. I count the pattern picks out loud as I weave. However, a useful tip if you have a floor loom is to have the plain weave background starting from the same side as your foot is on the treadle. For example, if you are lifting shafts 1 and 3 and throwing the shuttle from the right-hand side, make sure you are treadling with your right foot. Then the left foot treadles 2 and 4 when the plain weave shuttle is thrown from the left.

If you have a table loom, try to line up the handles that lift the shafts in the same manner. Right handles when you are throwing from right to left and vice versa. This way you can forget the actual shaft numbers for the plain weave picks, and just concentrate on the pattern picks. I think this tip has been the most useful thing to know in my long weaving life.

Weave 4 picks in plain weave (yellow) then 2 picks in the doubled blue pattern weft as before. Turn in the blue weft into the last pattern pick and cut off. Then weave 36cm (14in) in the background weft in plain weave. Repeat the blue stripes, the pattern border and the 2.5cm (1in) at the end of the mat. Hemstitch (page 95).

Pattern 1: Zigzags. Repeat the pattern four times. There will be 16 pattern picks with 16 plain weave picks in between each pattern pick. Add the last pattern pick on shafts 1 & 2 to balance the pattern.

Pattern 2: Diamonds. Weave the pattern twice, adding a last pick on shafts 1 & 2 to balance the pattern.

Pattern 3: More diamonds. Repeat the pattern twice. This pattern is written as 'Tromp as writ'. This is an expression used when the shaft lifting order is the same as the threading order. 'Tromp' is an old term for treadle. Again add a last pick on shafts 1 & 2 to balance the pattern.

Pattern 4: Elongated diamonds. Weave the pattern once. You will notice the same pick is repeated several times. This is possible because there is a plain weave pick in between. If this plain weave pick was absent, a repeated pick just undoes the one before.

Pattern 5: Woven on opposites, using shafts 1 & 2 and 3 & 4. Again the same pick is repeated several times with plain weave in between.

Pattern 6: More diamonds. Weave the pattern once.

After weaving each table mat, place a ruler (2.5cm/1in wide) across the warp in the shaft 1 & 3 shed, change to 2 & 4 and place a second ruler in this shed. This will leave a 5cm (2in) gap for the fringe. When you have woven a couple of centimetres (inches), take out the rulers. They do give you a firm edge to beat against for the first few picks and it is easier to remove two sticks rather than one wider stick.

Weave all six mats, remembering to hemstitch each end, and cut

7.4 It is possible to weave a wide variety of border patterns for table mats

the end mat off the loom, leaving a 2.5cm (1in) fringe. Unwind the mats from the front cloth beam and take out the heading picks by cutting the loops at each side, then pulling them out of the weaving. Undo the knots that attach the weaving to the front stick, and remove it from the loom. Cut the mats apart, and trim the first fringe to match. Check for mistakes. It is better to fix these now, and this is easier to do while the cloth is more open. Trim off any loose ends.

Washing: Put all the mats in the washing machine on the full cycle. I am tough when I wash articles like table mats that will have a hard life. If your spin cycle leaves creases in the cloth, drip-dry instead, then place the mats flat on a towel to dry. Press while slightly damp.

Variations

Cottolin is a good substitution for cotton. It is a blend of 60% cotton, 40% linen, size 22/2. The sett for this yarn would be 18–20 e.p.2.5cm (1in). The linen adds some firmness to the cloth, and there will be less shrinkage, hence the closer sett. See the cottolin runners in Chapter 4.

Linen is the classic yarn for table mats. It has some special qualities, so wait until you have some weaving experience before trying this yarn. Size 10/2 is a sensible thickness for table mats. Note the following points:

- It does not shrink. What you see on the loom is what you get, so beat firmly. Sett closer than you would for an equivalent cotton yarn, about 20–24 e.p.2.5cm (1in).

- It is inelastic. If you catch one of the warp ends with the shuttle and loosen that end, it will remain slack. So watch your shuttle throwing.

- Because the yarn is inelastic, when winding the warp onto the loom, make sure it is tightly wound around the warp beam. Don't let the warp slacken while winding.

- Washing: When linen cloth comes off the loom it is hard and looks rather thin and flimsy. Handwash in very hot water using lots of soap — a yellow laundry soap is ideal. Rub this soap well in with your hands, with the cloth placed on a washing board, if you have one, or the ribbed drainage portion of your kitchen sink. This will soften and full, or thicken, the linen. Rinse in hot water and gently (not hard as it will crease) squeeze the water out. Lay or hang the cloth until it stops dripping.

- Press under a cloth until dry. When it is dry, 'polish' the surface with a hot, dry iron directly onto the fabric to bring up the lustre of the linen.

- Do not store folded. Linen creases easily.

- A linen fringe is not a good idea as it will become raggedy very quickly. A hemmed end is best (page 107).

Ask yourself:

- Did I enjoy this project?
- What parts did I enjoy the most?
- What parts did I not enjoy doing?
- What did I learn?
- What can I improve about the finished project?

8.1 Cocoon front, black side

Reversible cocoon jacket

You will learn to weave a reversible cloth on four shafts

Minimum loom width: 61cm (24in). For a floor loom, you will need 8 treadles.

Cocoon jackets have been the favourite weaving projects for many weavers. The shape is simple with no cutting needed, and they drape beautifully if the right yarns are used. The fringes become an integral part of the garment, and one size fits most shapes and body sizes.

A cocoon looks like a shawl when worn but has the advantage that it will not slip off the shoulders because of the sleeve openings. I must have made hundreds of these; they sell readily and have never gone out of fashion.

By making the cloth reversible, you can have two garments for the price of one. The turned-back collar shows the reverse side when worn, adding interest to the garment.

Cocoons should be:
- soft next to the skin
- drape easily
- warm
- lightweight

CHARACTERISTICS

Soft: Because the cloth will touch your skin, the yarn should be soft. Any soft yarn is suitable, such as wool, mohair, silk, bamboo, Tencel or a soft, fluffy cotton. Because this cocoon will be woven in two rectangular strips which will later be joined, I have chosen fluffy yarns for the wefts so the seam down the centre back will be less obvious. At the end of this project, I will describe how to weave the cocoon in one piece on a wider loom so there is no need for the join.

Drape easily: The fabric should be flexible enough to drape around the body, rather like a shawl.

Warm: I like cocoons to be warm and light as well as decorative, as they are often worn as evening wear.

I have chosen a reversible structure, with two wefts, one in the top layer and one in the lower layer. The warp, which will not be seen in the finished garment, is a fine, soft wool, giving shape and strength to the cocoon. The top layer has a weft yarn that floats over three warp ends and under one, the lower layer does the same. Every fourth weft thread crosses over from the top to the lower layer, keeping the layers together,

8.2 Detail

so colours for each layer need to be such that the fourth thread is not noticeable on the other layer. For example, if I chose a white yarn for the top layer and a black yarn for the lower layer, that fourth thread would show up as a tiny spot on both layers. By choosing fluffy yarns, I can also obscure that crossing thread. This all sounds confusing at this stage but it will make sense when you start to weave.

The choice of colours is important. The warp yarn should be a neutral shade that will blend in with the weft colours. You can see by the photographs that the fringe in the finished garment is the warp yarn. I have chosen a black warp as the weft colours are dark. If the weft colours were pastel shades, I would have chosen a lighter warp colour.

I have been giving wraps per 2.5cm for each yarn used as then, if you can't get exactly the same yarn, you can use an equivalent. For fluffy yarns like mohair, it is difficult to get an exact number of wraps because of the fluffy bits. Do you push the yarns together or leave them more open? The wraps are accurate for the black wool used in the warp, as it is a plain yarn.

WARP PLAN

Warp yarn: 110/3 black wool, 9672m/kg (4800yd/lb)
Wraps: 30 per 2.5cm (1in)
Weft: Upper layer — purple brushed mohair, 1995m/kg (990yd/lb)
Wraps: 10 per 2.5cm (1in)
Weft: Lower layer — black looped mohair, 2015m/kg (1000yd/lb)
Wraps: 12 per 2.5cm (1in). This is the same yarn as used in Chapter 5.
Warp length: 2 rectangles 112cm (44in)
    + 30cm (12in) for fringes = 254cm (100in)
    Wastage = 91cm (36in)
    Total warp (rounded up) = 4m (13ft)
Weight of warp yarn required: Black wool = 300gm (10½oz)
Weight of weft yarn required: Purple brushed mohair = 300gm (10½oz), black looped mohair = 300gm (10½oz)
Width in reed: 61cm (24in) 384 ends
Sett: Warp 16 e.p.2.5cm (1in); weft 16 p.p.2.5cm (1in)
Reed: 8-dent
Woven length on loom: Each length 112cm (44in)
Threading: Straight draw 1, 2, 3, 4
Finished size after washing: 97cm (38in) x 60cm (23½in)
Finishing: Hemstitching
Structure: Reversible 1/3, 3/1 twill
Weight of finished cocoon: 480gm (17oz)
Winding the warp: Wind a warp 4m (13ft) long and 61cm (24in) wide. It will be quicker if you wind the warp with two ends at once as in page 62. Because this is a wool warp, which can be sticky, I suggest you wind with a cross at both ends, also on page 62. Because this is a wide warp, wind the warp in two sections, with 12 counting ties in each half. Remember to make all the ties in each half before you take

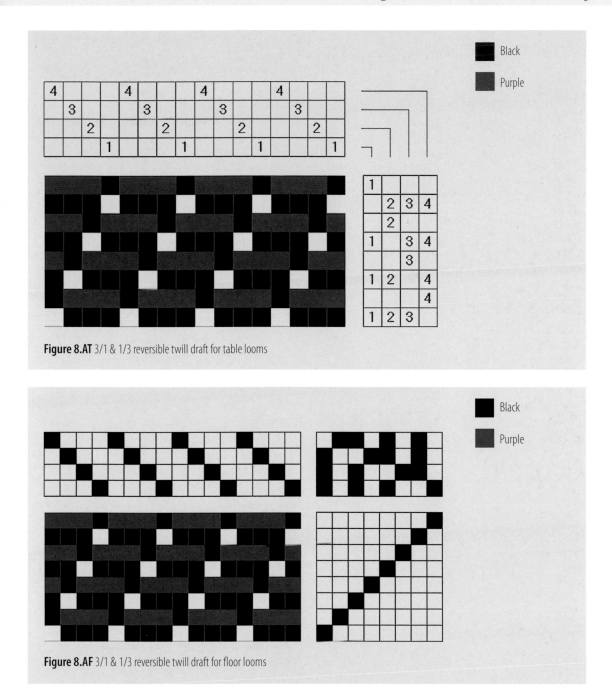

Figure 8.AT 3/1 & 1/3 reversible twill draft for table looms

Black

Purple

Figure 8.AF 3/1 & 1/3 reversible twill draft for floor looms

Black

Purple

the half warp off the warping board. Put a counting tie every 16 ends; 12 ties in each half.

Threading: Push 48 heddles on each shaft from the right-hand side to the centre. Thread with a straight draw: 1, 2, 3, 4. Every 16 ends, check, then tie with a slip knot. You should have 24 slip knots.

If you are using a floor loom, you will need 8 treadles, as there are 8 different lifts for each weft repeat. I have made this tie-up different from the other floor loom tie-ups, as it is easier simply to move your feet from right to left on the treadles as you weave.

Sleying: For an 8-dent reed, put 2 ends in each dent. If you have other reeds, see Appendix A, page 175. If you only have a 10-dent reed, sley for 15 ends per 2.5cm (1in).

Weaving: Weave the heading, lifting shafts 1 & 3, 2 & 4, and check the tension. Fill one shuttle with the black mohair yarn and the other shuttle with the purple yarn. Because these are thick yarns, stick or ski shuttles will hold the most yarn. Boat and end delivery shuttles are best used for finer, plain yarns.

Practice weaving: You will be weaving the first pick in the upper layer in the purple yarn (drafts 8.A, page 123). The second pick weaves the first black pick in the lower layer, the third pick weaves the upper purple layer again; the fourth pick weaves the second black pick in the lower layer. It all sounds confusing until you actually weave. Weave with a very light beat, just gently squeezing the beater against the fell of the cloth. You should see some light through the two layers. Remember the wool warp will shrink when it is washed and the weft will close up. If you beat heavily, you will have a very dense cloth and the cocoon will be inflexible. Eight of the top layer picks should equal approximately 2.5cm (1in). There is enough warp for you to practise for a few centimetres (inches) before you weave the cocoon lengths.

Place a stick across to separate the practice weaving from the actual cocoon lengths. Begin the first cocoon length by weaving for a couple of centimetres (inches), then hemstitch with the black warp yarn in groups of four. It is not fast weaving, as you are weaving two layers at once, but you get a two-sided garment so it is worth the extra time. On my jack loom, I had to push the lowered shafts down by hand with each pick because, as all the treadles are tied to some of the shafts, the shafts tend to rise when they shouldn't.

To make neat edges, don't join the two wefts at the selvedges. Always place the shuttle you have just finished weaving with behind the other shuttle on the fell of the cloth. This separates the two weft yarns at the selvedge. You will not be able to see the lower layer, although I usually take a peek underneath with a mirror just to see if I am doing it right. If you make a mistake and weave with the wrong shuttle in the wrong layer, it is easy to see this mistake straight away as the two colours are very different. The black warp just disappears among the fluffy yarns.

Weave the first half of the cocoon length for 112cm (44in), then hemstitch this end with the warp yarn. Leave a 15cm (6in) gap, and begin the second section of the cocoon, hemstitching the ends as before. When you have woven this section, hemstitch, leave 8cm (3in) of the warp for the last fringe and cut the cloth from the loom. Undo the heading and check and mend any mistakes. Cut the two sections apart, leaving the 8cm (3in) fringe at each end.

Washing: Wash the cloth in warm soapy water, rinse in warm water,

8.3 Cocoon back, purple side

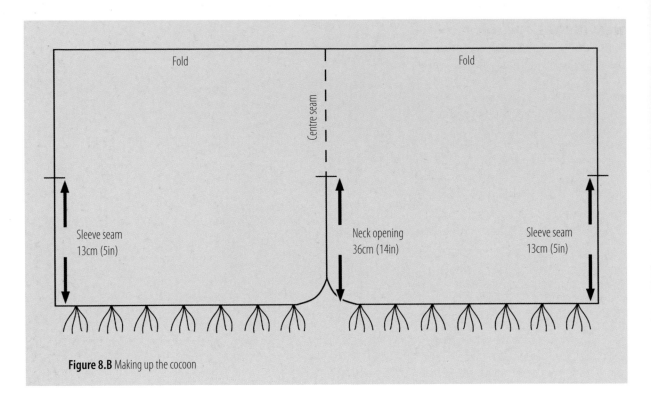

Fold

Fold

Centre seam

Sleeve seam
13cm (5in)

Neck opening
36cm (14in)

Sleeve seam
13cm (5in)

Figure 8.B Making up the cocoon

squeeze out the excess water and dry lying flat. Do not press as this will flatten the surface texture. Because I used a fine merino wool for the warp, the shrinkage rate in the length was high.

To make up: Using the black warp yarn and fine stitches, hand sew the two halves together on one long selvedge side, leaving 36cm (14in) open. Butt the two edges together rather than overlapping them, so the seam is flat.

Fold the two joined sections so the fringes are together, and join together for 13cm (5in) at the outside edges to form the armholes, as in figure 8.B. The back neck edge usually needs some reinforcing stitches. I always put my label here to strengthen this seam.

As the seam showed on the purple side (but not on the black), I twisted a braid with six lengths of the purple mohair and then doubled the length back on itself. The doubled length was sewn over the purple seam, from the lower edge to the neck. I then separated the twisted threads, with three each side, and re-twisted them to make a narrower braid which I sewed up the collar edgings. The tassels are an interesting finish to the braids. Depending on the texture of the weft yarn used, you may be able to hide the seams and the braiding will not be necessary.

When worn, the back neck edge should be about 10cm (4in) below the normal neck line, so the cocoon sits flat across the lower back edge. The front neck opening is folded back to form collars so the reverse side is showing.

WEAVING THE COCOON IN ONE PIECE

If your loom is 1.2m (4ft) or more wide, you can weave the cocoon in one piece. The warp width should be 1.2m (4ft) and the cloth is woven for 76cm (30in). At this point, mark the centre of the cloth with 60cm (23½in) each side by putting a thread through the reed. For the remaining 36cm (14in), weave with two shuttles at once. One shuttle (A) weaves the right side, the other (B) the left. Begin by putting the A shuttle through from the right side to the centre mark, take it out of the shed and lay it on the fell of the cloth. Then take shuttle B and, beginning at the centre mark, put this shuttle through from the centre to the left side. Beat. Change sheds and, starting with the left shuttle (B) return to the centre, place this shuttle on the fell of the cloth and pick up shuttle A from the centre and return to the right side. Beat. Do not build up one side more than the other as this means you can't use the beater.

When finishing off the cocoon, put some reinforcing stitches in at the point where you changed from one to two shuttles. There is no need for a centre seam when you weave this wider width.

8.4 Cocoon front, purple side

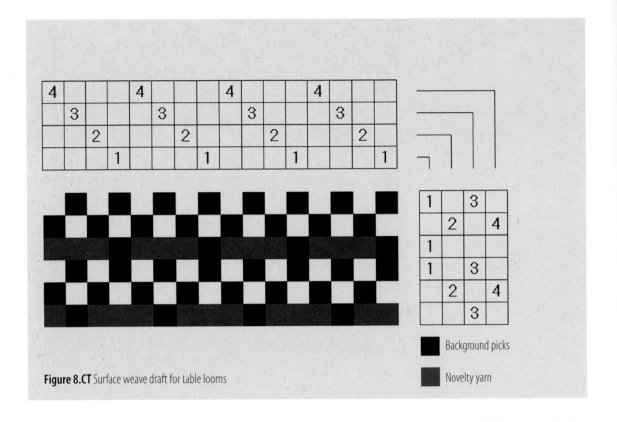

Figure 8.CT Surface weave draft for table looms

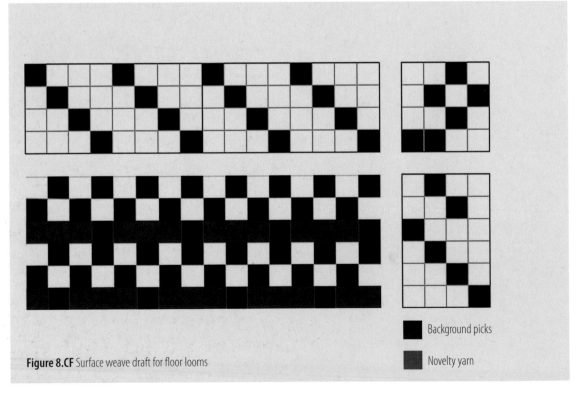

Figure 8.CF Surface weave draft for floor looms

8.5 (left) Surface weave cloth

8.6 Short pattern picks

Variations

There are many structures that can be woven for cocoons. You can weave a single layer, using the yarns and setts for the wrap in Chapter 5. If you are using a plain weave and yarn, the back seam will be more noticeable than if fluffy or textured yarns were used, and a braid, as described earlier, can be twisted and sewn over the back seam to hide it. A tassel on each end of the braid adds a decorative finish.

Surface weave

With the same threading used for this cocoon, you can also weave a surface weave structure (figures 8.CT and 8.CF and photo 8.5). The 2 plain weave background picks are woven in between each pattern weft. Begin with the same black yarn as the warp and weave 2 picks (1 & 3, 2 & 4) in plain weave. Then lift shaft 1 and weave with the purple mohair weft yarn. Then weave the 2 plain weave picks again followed by the purple weft, this time on shaft 3. This makes a firmer, lighter fabric than the reversible twill and has the advantage that it can be cut, as the background picks are effectively weaving a solid structure underneath the mohair weft.

The pattern picks don't have to continue from selvedge to selvedge; they can stop wherever you fancy, as the background wool weft, travelling from edge to edge, gives a firm structure all the way across. This is a very useful technique for building pattern blocks on a plain weave background.

Beginners guide to double weave

This reversible cloth is the beginning of a double-layer cloth. I can remember when I first discovered that, with four shafts, I could weave two layers at once. It seemed like magic to me. In this cocoon cloth, the two layers are joined every 4 warp ends. In double weave the layers are not joined. This is a useful technique if you want to weave cloth that is wider than your loom width, as you can join the two layers on one side to make a fold. You can also weave tubes by joining both sides. Or you can pick up parts of one layer and bring them through to the other layer. Complete books have been written on double weaves. One I have used for a long time is Ursina Arn-Grischott's *Doubleweave on Four to Eight Shafts*, published by Interweave Press, USA.

Ask yourself:

- Did I enjoy this project?
- What parts did I enjoy the most?
- What parts did I not enjoy doing?
- What did I learn?
- What can I improve about the finished project?

9.1 Cushions

Cushion covers

You will learn pick-up overshot

Minimum loom width: 46cm (18in)

Part of the secret of successful weaving is to be able to design so that the design fits the shape of the finished article. Sometimes I have seen cushions that look as if the weaver has woven a length of fabric, then cut it up to make a cushion. How much more exciting to be able to base the design on the shape of the cushion. The industrial weaving machines can't do individual pieces like this, but we can!

This cushion is square and I have outlined a square, then picked up an overshot pattern to fit inside the square. Overshot patterns usually extend from one selvedge to another, but we can place the pattern where we want it.

Cushions should be:
- comfortable to rest on
- flexible enough to have some give in the fabric
- hard-wearing

CHARACTERISTICS

Comfortable: Cushions should be comfortable to touch, sit on and lean against.

Flexible: Because a cushion cover has to fit around a cushion inner made of some type of stuffing, the fabric should be able to bend around the filling. Wool is the most flexible yarn of all, so is a good choice. It is not as washable as a cotton yarn, but cushions are not washed often and can be dry-cleaned.

Hard-wearing: Cushions are often sat on, thrown at the cat or spilt on, so they need to be hard-wearing. Do not choose a soft, fluffy yarn as it will pill (little balls forming on the surface) or show other signs of wear in a short time.

I have chosen a medium-weight wool with a reasonably tight twist. The twist will make for a hard-wearing fabric. The pattern yarn is slightly thicker than the background yarn as is usual with overshot patterns.

WARP PLAN

Warp yarn: Background — Tex 180/3 white wool, 2539m/kg (1260yd/lb)

Wraps: 20 per 2.5cm (1in)

Warp yarn: Pattern — green wool, 2015m/kg (1000yd/lb)

Wraps: 16 per 2.5cm (1in)

9.2 Cushion detail

131

Weft yarns: Same as warp
Warp length: 2 cushion covers 43cm (17in) square = 172cm (68in)
  Wastage = 91cm (36in)
  Total warp (rounded up) = 3m (10ft)
Weight of warp and weft yarn required: White wool = 370gm (13oz)
  Green wool = 100gm (3½oz)
Width in reed: 43cm (17in) 204 ends. If you want a larger cushion, add
  onto the side panels in multiples of 12.
Sett: 12 e.p.2.5cm (1in)
  12 p.p.2.5cm (1in)
Reed: 6 or 12 dent
Woven length on loom: Each cushion cover will be woven to 86cm
  (34in), with a gap in between. Hem allowance added.
Threading: Miniature monk's belt and straight draw
Finished size after washing: 39cm (15½in) square
Finishing: Hemstitching
Weight of one finished cushion cover: 125gm (4½oz)
Winding the warp: Wind a warp 3m (10ft) long. Wind the warp in
two sections with 102 ends in each. Make two crosses in the warp as
otherwise the wool ends will stick as you wind on (page 62).

Begin with the white yarn with 12 ends per 2.5cm (1in) for 10cm (4in).
Place the counting ties around every 12 ends. Then wind 10 ends in the
white and 2 ends in the green for the next 2.5cm (1in). Wind the next
18cm (7in) in the white again. Wind another 2 ends in the green and
10 in the white for 2.5cm (1in), followed by another 10cm (4in) in the
white, to give a total of 204 ends. Check this number carefully as you go
because we need the exact number in the centre square to make the
pattern balance. You should have 17 counting ties in all.

Threading: Push across 25 heddles from the right side (on each of
the four shafts) to the centre before you begin threading. Thread the
first 13cm (5in) in a straight draw: 1, 2, 3, 4. The last 2 ends will be in the
green pattern wool. Put a slip knot around every 12 ends (5 knots).

Then begin threading the miniature monk's belt pattern for the
next 18cm (7in), following drafts 9.A. There should be 84 ends in this
centre section. Thread the complete pattern four times, then add a
further 4 ends on shafts 1, 2, 3, 4. This is a repeat of the first 4 ends
in the pattern. If these extra ends aren't added, the pattern will look
uneven (it makes sense when you see it). Put a slip knot around every
20 ends for the first three pattern repeats, and another slip knot
around the last 24 ends (4 slip knots). Then complete the threading
with the final 13cm (5in) in a straight draw: 1, 2, 3, 4 (5 knots).

If you find your counting was incorrect when you wound the warp
and you run out of ends, you can add extra ends to save re-doing the
whole thing (page 59). Cut off 3m (10ft) of warp yarn and just add this
end into the warp as an extra end. One end is tied to the front rod
and the other end is weighted and hung off the back of the loom as
you weave. You will have to get up every now and then to move the

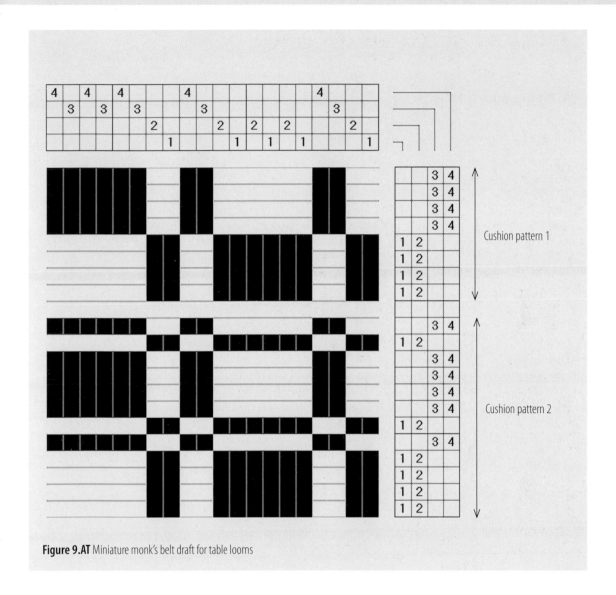

Figure 9.AT Miniature monk's belt draft for table looms

weight further down as you weave. Hopefully, as I have done all the calculations for you, you won't need these extra ends.

Sleying: Use a 12-dent reed and place 1 end in each dent. With a 6-dent reed, place 2 ends in each dent. If you have another reed size, consult the chart in Appendix A, page 175.

Weaving: I have given you two versions of the pattern. The first version is easier to follow, so begin with this one. The second cushion can be a repeat of the first, or you can try the second version. Version two takes a bit more concentration.

Cushion 1: Weave a heading (page 56), place a ruler across to leave a gap for the hemstitching, then begin weaving the first cushion. Weave with 12 picks to 2.5cm (1in). Hemstitch in threes after you have woven about 2–3cm (1in).

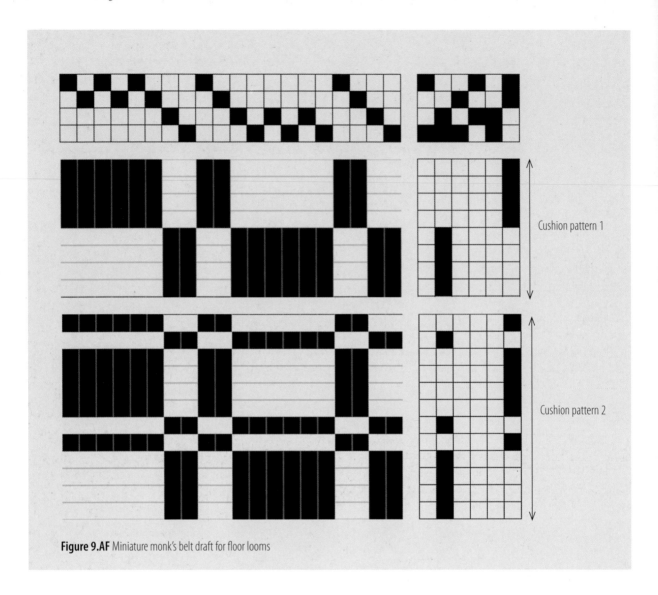

Cushion pattern 1

Cushion pattern 2

Figure 9.AF Miniature monk's belt draft for floor looms

Measure the width from the selvedge to one of the green stripes, and weave this same amount in the white wool in a plain weave: 1 & 3, 2 & 4, plus 2.5cm (1in) extra for the hem allowance. The warp is always stretched tighter on the loom than the weft so, to allow for the contraction once the fabric is removed from the loom, always weave 2–3 picks more in the weft than in the warp.

Place 2 picks of the green weft across, also in plain weave. Break off the green weft, tucking the ends into the shed. See page 112 for a neat way to finish off these 2 picks without doubled, turned-in edges.

There is a plain weave pick in between each pattern pick (pattern 1 on drafts in figures 9.AT, page 133, and 9.AF), and this white plain weave continues from selvedge to selvedge. Begin by weaving the first plain weave pick on shafts 1 & 3, selvedge to selvedge. Then lift the

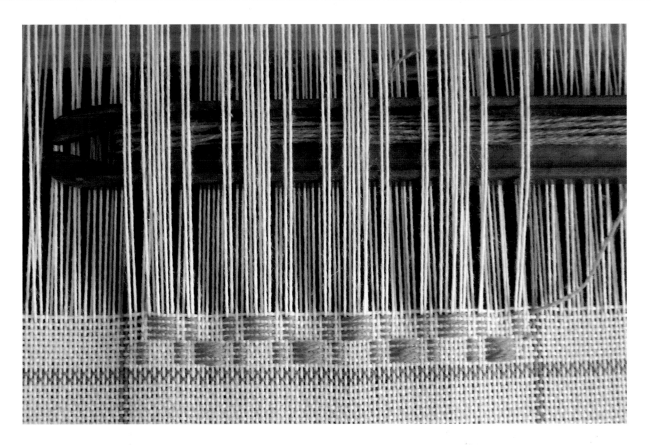

9.3 Inserting the pattern shuttle

first pattern pick of 3 & 4, and insert the shuttle, holding the green weft down, between the green stripe and the pattern area into the open shed. Bring the shuttle up when you reach the other green stripe. The pattern weft doesn't touch the green stripes. Tuck the beginning of the green weft into the same shed.

Weave the next plain weave pick of 2 & 4 with the background (white) weft, from selvedge to selvedge, then the next pattern pick of 3 & 4. Finish this block by repeating the pattern pick of 3 & 4 twice more, with the background in between. The plain weave picks in between the pattern picks are often called the 'tabby binder' and you will see this written on some drafts. If you see this notation, you know to add plain weave picks in between.

You will notice as you weave the pattern area that the edges look untidy as you are bringing the green weft up for the next pick because the green yarn curves slightly. Don't worry about this as this is the wrong side of the weaving. When we make up the cushions the underside of the weaving will be the right, neat side. If you don't believe me, take a look when the weaving has progressed enough for you to see the underside and you will see how neat it really is.

Continue weaving like this, following treadling draft 1, until the centre square measures 18cm (/in). Finish at the end of one block, not in the middle. This ensures the beginning and end will match. Finish with a plain weave pick, then 2 picks of plain weave in the green from selvedge to selvedge to outline the pattern area. The pattern square should be slightly higher than wider to allow for contraction when the weaving is taken from the loom.

Weave for another 13cm (5in) in plain weave in the white. This will finish off the first side of the cushion. Put a short piece of wool in the selvedge to mark the end of the first cushion side, then weave another 13cm (5in) in the white for the other side of the cushion.

Repeat the green pattern square, then finish off the cushion with the white wool as for the first side, remembering to add the hem allowance of 2.5cm (1in) and hemstitch.

Place a ruler across to leave a gap or about 5cm (2in) before you begin the second cushion.

Cushion 2: This pattern is written as 'Tromp as writ', as the treadling sequence is the same as the threading. See Appendix D, pages 182–83, for more details on this type of treadling.

Weave with the same measurements as in the first cushion. The pattern square will be woven with five-and-a-half repeats of pattern 2, or until the centre square measures 18cm (7in), finishing on the eighth pattern pick with a 2 & 4 to balance the pattern. This ensures the beginning and end will match. Finish with a plain weave pick, then 2 picks of plain weave in the green to outline the pattern area. Again the pattern square should be slightly higher than wider to allow for contraction when the weaving is taken from the loom.

Hemstitch the end of the second cushion, then cut the fabric from the loom, leaving a fringe of about 2.5cm (1in). Cut the two cushion lengths apart.

Washing: Wash the cushions by hand in warm soapy water, rinse and lay flat to dry. Press while slightly damp.

Staying on track

Because you are weaving with two shuttles, each shuttle weaving a different structure, it is easy to get muddled. A good way to keep track of which shuttle is doing what is to always begin from the same side when weaving the plain weave shafts from selvedge to selvedge. I try to line up my feet (on a floor loom) and the handles (on a table loom) with the shuttle. For example, if I am throwing the shuttle from the right to the left for the 1 & 3 pick, I use my right treadle or handle. If I am throwing the shuttle from the left, I use my left treadle or handle. This way it is much harder to make a mistake. This is one of the most useful tricks I ever learnt.

To make up: Purchase a cushion inner the correct size. Fold the cushion in half lengthwise, butt the sides together, match up the green stripes and sew the edges together with the white wool. Turn over a hem on the open end (you may need to trim the fringe closer to the weaving first). There are various ways of finishing this end. A zip closure or velcro can be used, and sometimes I just sew the hemmed-under ends together after the cushion insert is placed inside. When I wash the cushion it is easy to unpick this stitching. It all depends on how often you will be washing the cushion cover. If you finish with a braid, as below, you may have to remove this before taking out the cushion inner before washing the cover.

Braiding: Because the four sides of the cushion have different edges, one folded and the others sewn, braiding adds a good finishing touch.

9.4a (top) **& b** (bottom) Finger crochet

137

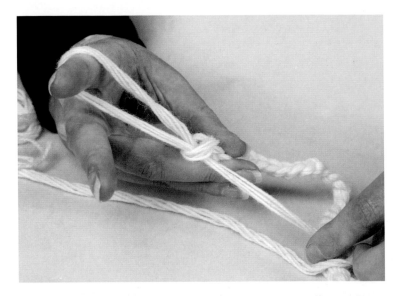

9.4c (top) **& d** (bottom) Finger crochet

A finger crocheted braid in the white wool is easy to do (photos 9.4a, b, c and d). Measure out 6 lengths 10m (11yd) long. To make this long length easier to handle while you are finger crocheting, chain the length, as on page 42. Make a slip knot loop in one end and put this loop over your left thumb or forefinger (if you are right-handed; reverse if left-handed).

Take the next section of the yarn and place this over the left thumb or forefinger, in front of the slip knot loop, then with the other hand take the first loop over this section. Pull the length hanging down to slide the loop tight. You need a firm braid so give a strong tug to this length. Continue doing this for the necessary length. One side is flatter than the other and this is the side you sew around the cushion edges. It is impossible to join the braid, so make sure you have enough for all four cushion sides.

Knot both ends, make a tassle and sew the braid onto the cushion, beginning with the top side, the last side you closed. Sew the braid right around the cushion, including the folded end, and close with another tassel where the two ends met.

Variations

To outline the pattern in these cushions, I have only threaded the pattern in the centre panel. This does take some careful calculations before you start, which I have done for you. However, you can thread the entire width in the pattern and then you are free to place pattern squares wherever you want across the width.

You need to be careful where you pick up, to make neat pattern edges, but this approach gives you lots of freedom. A fellow weaver once wove a beautiful altar cloth with random sections picked up.

It took me many years of weaving before I realised that I didn't have to weave a pattern from selvedge to selvedge. This freedom is something industrial looms haven't got so we should make the most of it.

Ask yourself:

- Did I enjoy this project?
- What parts did I enjoy the most?
- What parts did I not enjoy doing?
- What did I learn?
- What can I improve about the finished project?

10.1 Scarf

Scarf

You will learn wandering warp ends

Minimum loom width: 25cm (10in)

Every now and then in my weaving life there would come moments when I realised the limits of the loom could be overcome by some lateral thinking. Because I was mainly self-taught, I discovered these techniques for myself, which was more exciting than if I had been taught them by a teacher.

Nothing is new in weaving because it is such an ancient craft, but I felt as though I had discovered the wheel all by myself when I realised the warp and weft could be interchanged. This interchange is excellent for scarves because the pattern can run the length of the scarf. It is also ideal for production weaving because each scarf can have its own different 'wandering warps'.

Scarves should be
- soft
- flexible
- lightweight

CHARACTERISTICS

Shape: I usually make my scarves a long, narrow rectangle. I like to place the pattern either as a border at each end, as this is what shows when the scarf is worn, or running the length of the scarf.

Soft: Any soft yarn can be used for a scarf. I have chosen Tencel for this scarf, but it could be woven in wool, softly spun cotton, bamboo or silk, to name just a few. One criteria is that the wandering warp ends should be of a similar material as the rest of the warp. If these ends shrink to a different length than the body of the scarf, you will get a crinkly effect. To match the Tencel, I have chosen a rayon ribbon for the wandering warps.

Lightweight: Warm winter scarves can be heavier than lightweight summer scarves, but both should be flexible enough to fold easily around your neck. Because scarves don't have the wear and tear of garments such as jackets, skirts, etc., I usually sett the warp ends slightly further apart.

The wandering warps are ends that are added into the warp after the background warp is on the loom. They are threaded in the same heddle and reed dent as a background warp, and weighted at the back of the loom (photo 10.2, page 143). When the wandering warp ends

141

need to be turned into a weft pick, they are removed from the weight, heddle and reed, placed in the shed as a weft pick and then returned to another heddle and reed dent, where they become warp ends again. A 2/2 twill structure, with its over two, under two intersections, will allow the pattern yarn to show through more than a plain weave, which goes over and under one warp end.

WARP PLAN
Warp yarn: Background — variegated 8/2 Tencel, 6770m/kg (3360yd/lb)
Wraps: 40 per 2.5cm (1in)
Warp yarn: Wandering warp yarns — variegated rayon ribbon
Wraps: 3 per 2.5cm (1in)
Weft yarn: Same as the warp
Warp length: Scarf: 183cm (72in)
   + 24cm (9½in) for fringes = 207cm (81½in)
   Wastage = 91cm (36in)
   Total warp (rounded up) = 3m (10ft)
Weight of warp and weft yarn required: Tencel = 200gm (7oz)
   Rayon ribbon = 15m (16½yd)
Width in reed: 23cm (9in) 216 ends
Sett: 24 e.p. 2.5cm (1in)
   24 p.p. 2.5cm (1in)
Reed: 8 or 12 dent
Woven length on loom: 183cm (72in)
Threading: Straight draw
Structure: 2/2 twill
Finished size after washing: 170cm (67in) by 22cm (8½in)
Finishing: Hemstitched with twisted fringe
Weight of finished scarf: 130gm (4½oz)
Winding the warp: Wind a warp 3m (10ft) long and 23cm (9in) wide. Because Tencel is a slippery thread, one cross at one end will be sufficient. Just wind the Tencel yarn; the ribbon will be added later. Put a counting tie around every 24 ends and, because this yarn is slippery, put in several choke ties. There will be 9 counting ties.
Threading: Push across 27 heddles from the right-hand side to the centre and thread with a straight draw: 1, 2, 3, 4. Put a slip knot around every 24 ends (9 slip knots). When you get to the centre, just take the heddles from the left side; you don't need to push them across first.
Sleying: With an 8-dent reed, place 3 ends in each dent. With a 12-dent reed, place 2 in each dent. If you have other reeds, see Appendix A, page 175. Tie the warp onto the front rod.
Placing the ribbons: Measure out three lengths of ribbon, each 5m (16½ft) long. Do not stint with this length as if you run out of ribbon before you reach the end you will have a short scarf, and there needs to be plenty left at the end of the scarf so the weights can hang over the back beam.

10.2 Weighting the pattern warp ends

Take each ribbon through a heddle and a reed dent with one of the Tencel ends. I place the ribbons through the heddle eyes on shaft 1 every time, as this is the shaft nearest to me when I weave and the easiest to reach. Tie these ribbon ends onto the front rod. Weight each ribbon at the back of the loom, so they are the same tension as the rest of the warp. I use large bulldog clips, which I can easily clip onto the ribbon.

Weaving: Weave a heading, then leave a small gap and begin weaving a 2/2 twill (figures 3.DT and 3.DF, page 82). Because the Tencel is slippery, you may need to tie a bow on top of the knot at the front rod to prevent the surgeon's knot from coming undone. If the bow leaves a bump as you wind the front rod on, place a narrow piece of cardboard over the bumps to prevent this affecting the tension.

Weave for about 5cm (2in). Hemstitch in fours. Remember that the Tencel will not change much with washing, so what you see on the loom is how the cloth will look once it is off the loom. A firm beat is best. Remove the weight from one of the ribbons and take it

143

10.3 Changing the ribbons from warp to weft

out of the heddle and reed dent. Pull the whole length through to the front of the loom and open the next shed. Position the ribbon where you want it to go, then take it out of the shed and re-thread it back through the reed and heddle eye in the new position. It will pull up towards the reed but don't worry, the next pick will place it correctly. Reattach the weight and carry on weaving, following the 2/2 twill sequence.

Place the pattern ribbons wherever you fancy. I always make a feature of the beginning and end of a scarf, as this is where the pattern will show most when the scarf is worn. The fun thing about this is that you can play with the ribbon patterns anywhere. It is a bit fiddly changing the ribbons from the warp to the weft then back again, but if you use threading and reed hooks to replace the ribbons, it doesn't take long. Because my Baby Wolf loom is short from front to back, I can do all the ribbon rearranging without getting up and going to the back of the loom. With a bigger loom, you will have to get out of your seat to detach and re-attach the weights.

When you have woven 183cm (72in), hemstitch the end and cut the scarf from the loom, leaving about 12cm (5in) for the fringe.

Twist the Tencel ends of the fringe (figure 11.A, page 151). Trim the ribbons to the same length as the twisted fringe after washing, as this makes a neater ribbon end.

Washing: Hand wash the scarf in warm soapy water, rinse, then lay flat to dry. Press while still slightly damp with the iron on the setting for rayon yarns (not too hot).

10.4 Scarf detail

Variations

Any fancy yarns can be used for the wandering wefts, as long as they are the same type of yarn as the body of the scarf. For example, for a wool scarf, the ribbons should also be wool. This means they will shrink the same amount. I collect odd balls of fancy yarns from sale bins.

Ask yourself:

- Did I enjoy this project?
- What parts did I enjoy the most?
- What parts did I not enjoy doing?
- What did I learn?
- What can I improve about the finished project?

11.1 Scarf

Ruffle scarf

You will learn how to use elastic yarns

Minimum loom width: 25cm (10in)

Scarves are always popular, not only because you can use a small, narrow loom, but also because they are a useful accessory which makes a great gift.

For a long time I have been intrigued with the result of using yarns that behave differently. In the beginning this was usually an accident. Once I wove some tartan fabric without realizing that one of the yarns was wool, the other acrylic. Nothing happened to warn me while I was weaving, but when I washed the fabric, one shrank, the other didn't and the more I washed and pressed the cloth to make it lie flat, the more crinkly it became.

When I knew more about yarns, I used this differential shrinkage to make many interesting fabrics and eventually I wrote a book on the subject (*Collapse Weave: Creating Three-Dimensional Cloth*). There are many interesting yarns coming on the market all the time and each new type of yarn opens up new adventures for the weaver. The fun part of weaving these collapse fabrics is that the real beauty doesn't show up until after the fabric is washed, as the end result looks nothing like the cloth on the loom.

Scarves should be:
- soft
- flexible
- lightweight

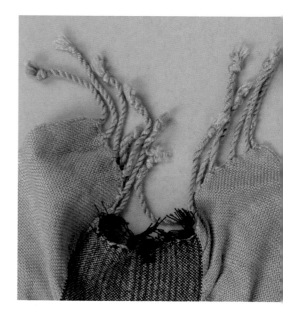

11.2 Detail of scarf fringe

CHARACTERISTICS

Shape: Scarves can be any shape but they are usually a long, narrow rectangle. I like my scarves to be long enough to go around my neck a couple of times, which also makes them long enough to do fancy ties in the front. This collapse weave scarf can also be worn like a ruffle.

Soft: Wool, loosely woven cottons, silk, Tencel or bamboo are good yarn choices as they will feel soft, not prickly next to your skin. If you are doubtful about whether a yarn is soft enough, rub some strands under your chin. Merino is a good choice for a wool yarn as it is the softest and finest of the wool breeds.

Flexible: A scarf should be flexible enough to wrap around your neck and not be too bulky when knotted or folded. When worn, this collapse scarf has the folds running down the length of the scarf, so this horizontal movement makes the scarf hang well.

Lightweight: Scarves are worn for decoration and/or warmth. Even if a scarf is worn mainly for warmth, it should not be heavy as a solid scarf will not comfortably fit around your neck. I sett scarves further apart than I would for other fabrics that will get more wear and tear. For example, a yarn I would sett at 24 e.p.2.5cm (1in) for a balanced weave vest or jacket, I would sett at 16 for a scarf. A balanced weave is one where there are the same number of warp ends to weft picks per centimetre (inch). If I sett the warp ends at 16, I would also weave with 16 picks per 2.5cm (1in).

The structure I have chosen for this scarf is one where the centre stripe is in colcolastic, with the outside stripes in bamboo. Colcolastic is a cotton/Lycra blend that pulls in a lot when it is washed. It is 93% cotton and 7% Lycra. Because of the high cotton content, the yarn behaves like normal yarn until it is washed, although I have found that if the humidity is high, the colcolastic tends to wrinkle up as some moisture will enter the yarn. When it is under tension on the loom, it behaves like normal yarn.

The outside stripes in bamboo will not shrink but the colcolastic centre stripe will contract when the tension is released and when the scarf is washed. This pulls the outside bamboo stripes into ruffles. The most important thing is to choose a yarn for the centre stripe that is shrinkable.

Bamboo is a lovely, luxurious yarn which is relatively new on the market. It drapes well, is soft, smooth and lustrous, and doesn't shrink. It has many of the characteristics of silk but is less slippery and easier to use for beginner weavers. Tencel would also be a good choice.

Both warp yarns can be wound onto one beam. For yarns that behave very differently on the loom, and when warping long warps, it is advisable to use two warp beams. However, for a short warp such as this one, we can wind the two yarns in this warp on one beam. To allow for the contraction when washed, weave the scarf longer than normal.

WARP PLAN

The centre stripe in colcolastic will be 8cm (3in) wide, with a 8cm (3in) wide stripe in bamboo either side.

The 10/2 bamboo I have chosen for this project wraps around a ruler for 40 wraps per 2.5cm (1in). Therefore the normal sett would be half this for a balanced weave. Remember when you wind the yarn for an inch, half of this will be warp and half weft, so a correct warp sett is half, hence the 20. Because this yarn will not shrink at all and is slippery, I have sett it slightly closer at 24 e.p.2.5cm (1in).

The colcolastic is a fine thread with 48 wraps to the inch. I have sett this yarn at 32 e.p.2.5cm (1in).

Warp yarn: Black colcolastic for centre stripe, Nm 34/2. One mini spool holds 50gm (1¾oz)

Wraps: 48 per 2.5cm (1in)

Warp yarn: 10/2 teal bamboo for side stripes, 8463m/kg (4200yd/lb)

Wraps: 40 per 2.5cm (1in)
Weft yarn: Bamboo, same as warp
Warp length: Scarf: 213cm (84in)
    + 20cm (8in) for fringes = 233cm (92in)
    Wastage = 91cm (36in)
    Total warp (rounded up) = 3.5m (11½ft)
Weight of warp and weft yarns required: Colcolastic = 10gm (½oz)
    Bamboo = 200gm (7oz)
Width in reed: 23cm (9in) 240 ends
Sett: Centre stripe in colcolastic, 32 e.p.2.5cm (1in)
    Outside stripes in bamboo, 24 e.p.2.5cm (1in)
    Because we are using one reed for 2 different setts, the reed size
    must be compatible with both.
Reed: 8 or 12-dent
Woven length on loom: 213cm (84in)
Threading: Straight draw
Structure: Plain weave
Finished size after washing: 127cm (50in)
Finishing: Hemstitching
Weight of finished scarf: 100gm (3½oz)
Winding the warp: Wind a warp 3.5m (11½ft) long with two crosses (page 62), otherwise the yarns will stick on the cross sticks. Wind the first 8cm (3in) with the bamboo, with 24 ends in each 2.5cm (1in), 72 ends. The counting ties will be around each 24 ends. Then wind another 8cm (3in) in colcolastic, with 32 ends in each 2.5cm (1in), 96 ends. Do not pull the colcolastic tight when winding. Follow with another 8cm (3in) in bamboo as before (72 ends). There should be 9 counting ties when you have finished. Use lots of choke ties. The warp will shrivel up when it is taken off the warping board, as the colcolastic contracts but it will behave itself once it is under tension and on the loom. The amount of contraction depends on the humidity, i.e., the more moisture in the air, the more is absorbed into the colcolastic and the more it contracts.
Threading: Push across 30 heddles on the first four shafts from the right-hand side to the centre. Thread 1, 2, 3, 4 for the complete width in both the colcolastic and bamboo, checking and tying each 2.5cm (1in) group of ends in a slip knot.

    The colcolastic has a mind of its own so here are some hints for threading this yarn through the heddles.

- This section needs patience. Luckily it is only 8cm (3in) wide. And once you have used this type of yarn, you will appreciate how easy other yarns are to use!
- Remember that the colcolastic needs to be under tension to stop it tangling.
- Leave long lengths of yarn in front of the heddles after you have wound the warp onto the back beam. If you leave short lengths, the colcolastic will slip back through the heddle after threading.

11.3 Scarf on loom under tension

- Only cut the loops at the end of the colcolastic section of the warp when you are ready to begin this section. I usually cut this part of the warp in three parts, not all at once. This helps with the tangling.
- When you have threaded 2.5cm (1in), check carefully and make sure each end is through the heddle and has not sprung back. There will be 9 slip knots.

Sleying: 8-dent reed: Place the bamboo ends 3 per dent (24 e.p.2.5cm (1in), and the colcolastic ends 4 per dent (32 e.p.2.5cm (1in)). 12-dent reed: Place the bamboo ends 2 in each dent and the colcolastic ends 2-3-3 (as in Appendix A, page 175.)

Tying on: Make sure the colcolastic ends are all included and haven't sneaked back through the reed while you weren't looking. Do not stretch the colcolastic ends when you tie on.

Weaving: When you have woven the heading, check the tension is even all the way across and adjust the surgeon's knot if necessary. The colcolastic section will feel stretchy. Bamboo is slippery, so once the tension is even, tie a bow on top of the surgeon's knot to keep the bamboo ends from loosening as you weave.

Weave a heading, then fill a shuttle with the bamboo yarn used in the warp. You may want to weave for a few centimetres (inches) to get the beat right before you begin the scarf proper. Weave a plain weave, lifting 1 & 3, 2 & 4 alternately with 24 p.p.2.5cm (1in). The bamboo yarn will not change much when it comes off the loom; what you see on the loom is what the finished cloth will look like, so beat firmly.

When the beat looks correct, place a stick across to leave a gap for the hemstitching, and begin the scarf. Hemstitch with the bamboo after you have woven a few centimetres (inches) in groups of six. Weaving is the easy part with this project. Once you have the colcolastic under control, it behaves like any other yarn.

Weave for 214cm (84in), then hemstitch this end and cut the scarf from the loom, leaving 10cm (4in) on the end for the fringe. Remove the heading. Finish the fringes by twisting the bamboo sections, then tie an overhand knot (page 86) on each twisted end. If you leave the twisting until after washing, you will find the ends become tangled. For the colcolastic ends, which will crumple up into little fuzzy balls as you take the scarf off the loom, just tie an overhand knot close to the hemstitching, and cut the ends about 3–5cm (1–2in) close to the knot.

Finishing: As soon as the centre colcolastic stripe hits the water it collapses. Hand wash in hot water, rinse and lie flat to dry. Press the bamboo stripes while slightly damp. Stretch the scarf out so the bamboo stripes on either side are flat. Iron the bamboo sides, but not the elastic centre.

A **fringe twister** is a clever device which makes a clockwise twist by turning the handle one way and an anticlockwise twist by turning it the other way.

11.4 Fringe twister

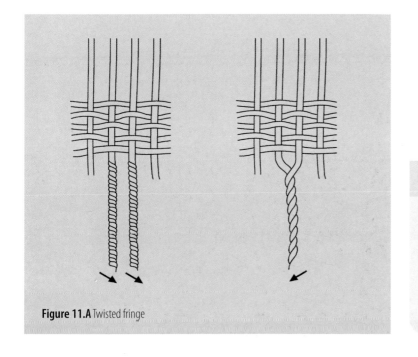

Figure 11.A Twisted fringe

Ask yourself:

- Did I enjoy this project?
- What parts did I enjoy the most?
- What parts did I not enjoy doing?
- What did I learn?
- What can I improve about the finished project?

12.1 Floor rug detail
12.2 Floor rug

Weft-faced floor rug

Woven by Jane Clark

You will learn how to weave a floor rug

Minimum loom size: 76cm (30in)

The very first floor rug I wove went well. The warp was covered by the weft, the thickness was right and the selvedges were perfect. I also had the correct type of loom for rug weaving, not that I knew that at the time. It was all a matter of luck as I didn't know what I was doing. Consequently, the second floor rug was a mess: the warp showed through and it was too thin. I didn't realise then that the relationship in size between the warp and weft yarns was important, so I was just lucky for the first rug that, by accident, I chose the correct size yarns. It took me four practice rugs before I wove one that I was happy enough to sell.

Floor rugs should be:
- strong
- hard-wearing
- colour fast
- non-slip

CHARACTERISTICS

Strong and hard-wearing: These all-important characteristics are the product of decisions you need to make before beginning your rug project such as what yarn to use, the type of loom on which the rug will be woven, and the tension system and weaving structure you will use. I cover these in aspects in more detail on pages 154–56.

Colour fast: Because rugs are usually exposed to sunlight, the colour should be fast. I recommend using commercial rug/carpet yarn as this very colour fast.

Non-slip: Rugs that move on the floor are dangerous so they need to be heavy enough to stay put. To prevent the edges curling, which can also cause falls, rugs must lie flat. Weaving a correct heading, which will be covered on page 158, ensures the edges lie flat.

Size: There is no set size for floor rugs — I have seen handwoven floor runners that are 4m (13ft) long. However, if you are not weaving a floor rug for a specific space, a well-proportioned rug will look best if the length is twice the width.

YARN

Because we walk on floor rugs, they need to stand up to a lot of wear. The yarns used should be very hard-wearing both in the warp and the weft. Two or three-ply rug (also called carpet) wool is a good choice for the weft as this has been worsted spun for carpet weaving and is very durable. Worsted spun yarn is from long fibres, arranged in a parallel formation when spinning. Depending on the thickness required, two, three or four strands of this yarn are used together. Rug wool usually comes from a coarse breed of sheep, such as Scottish Blackface or, in New Zealand, Drysdale. These are long-wool sheep whose fleeces usually contain some kemp (short, hair-like fibres).

Earlier I mentioned the relationship between the warp and the weft yarns in rugs. The thicker the warp, the thinner the weft will need to be to cover the warp. So the warp needs to be thick enough to make a strong base for the rug, but still able to be covered by a weft thick enough to be solid and hard-wearing. Rug wool is a special type of wool, and I have given a list of suppliers in Appendix B, page 178.

The wool used in this rug is a two-ply rug wool, 11 wraps to 2.5cm (1in), used with two strands at once. The advantage with using a thinner wool and multiple strands is that you can vary the colours in your rug by blending the strands to give you a wide range.

Rug wools come in various weights and plies, so you will have to experiment at the beginning of the rug to see how many strands you will need to completely cover the warp. I have allowed for this sampling in the warp length for this project. As your rug wool may be a different size to the one I have used in this rug, wrap it around a ruler to get the wraps per 2.5cm (1in), and compare this to my yarn. Then judge the number of strands accordingly.

For the warp I prefer linen, as this is very strong, slippery and inelastic. The slippery part is important as the weft has to completely cover the warp for this type of weaving, and a slippery warp allows the weft to slide down more easily when beating. Another advantage of using a linen warp yarn is that the natural colour of the linen blends in with any weft colour. A very tightly plied cotton warp (often called seine twine) is my second choice. The warp should be inelastic with no give in it, again allowing the weft to slide down. The edges of the rug will be strengthened with a thickened selvedge.

LOOM

The choice of loom is very important. Understandably, the loom must be solid and strong enough to withstand the heavy beating needed for floor rugs. But the shaft-lifting mechanism is just as important. A rising shed loom, such as a jack or a table loom, can't give the strong warp tension required. If the warp is not under a constant tension, the weft will not pack down sufficiently. The warp should have no give in it; therefore countermarch or counterbalance looms are best for this type of weaving.

12.3 Rug beater

A rising shed loom, such as a jack or table loom, has the lower shed layer pulled down at an angle below the horizontal line between the back and breast beam. When the shed is opened, the upper layer must rise to the same extent as the lower layer is dropped. If this does not happen, the warp in the upper shed will be tighter than the lower layer and the weft does not pack down properly. See figures 1.D and 1.E in Chapter 1, pages 21 and 22.

Because the rug warp is very strong and inelastic, on a rising shed loom, the lower warp will pull upwards to the horizontal position when the shed is opened and the two layers are then under a different tension. With countermarch and counterbalance looms, both layers move apart the same distance regardless of the warp strength because the treadle action is positive, pulling some shafts up and the opposing shafts down simultaneously.

There are vertical rug looms, usually two-shaft, but mostly these are best suited for tapestry weaving, as the beating may not be heavy enough for a floor rug unless a weighted rug beater is used. The beater in photo 12.3 weighs 610gm (21½oz).

TENSION SYSTEM

Because the warp must be under a continuous tight tension, a ratchet and pawl system is usually the best as, with a taut linen warp, there should be no give. I found that I also needed a strong turning handle with spokes to get the warp under enough tension. See Chapter 2, photo 2.22, page 48 for more information.

The other type of brake, a friction brake with a spring, cable and brake drum, does not usually give sufficient tension for such a strong warp.

All the above information may be daunting to a beginner. If you decide you want to weave more than two or three floor rugs, you will need a loom as previously described. However, if you want to try weaving a rug just to see if you like this sort of weaving, use the loom you have and make the best of it. Table looms are too lightweight, but if you have a rising shed floor loom, use a strong cotton warp — as this has some elasticity — not a linen warp thread, and you will be able to weave an adequate rug. It may not be as strong or as hard-wearing as a rug woven on a linen warp on a countermarch or counterbalance loom, but you will have some fun.

If you are serious about weaving rugs, the best advice I can give is to acquire *The Techniques of Rug Weaving* by Peter Collingwood. This book was first printed in 1968 but has had many editions since then and is the bible of rug weaving.

STRUCTURE

A weft-face structure, where the weft completely covers the warp, makes for a strong, hard-wearing rug. This is made by spacing the warp ends sufficiently so the weft will curve completely around each warp end, as in figures 2.A and 2.B, page 38. Earlier I mentioned the relationship between the warp and the weft yarns. The thicker the warp, or the closer the sett, the thinner the weft will need to be to cover the warp. This always seemed the wrong way around to me, but it works. There is also a weaving technique, described later in this chapter, called 'bubbling the weft' which covers the warp well.

WARP PLAN

Warp yarn: Linen 8/5 881m/kg (437yd/lb)
   Or linen 8/6 812m/kg (403yd/lb)
   If you cannot source these linen yarns, a strong, tightly twisted cotton (seine twine) about the same size is adequate as a second choice.
Warp length: Rug, including fringes = 180cm (71in)
   Wastage = 91cm (36in)
   Total warp (allowing extra for practice) = 3m (10ft)
Weft yarn: 2-ply rug wool in colours ranging from black to pale blue.
   11 wraps per 2.5cm (1in). Used twofold.
Weight of warp and weft yarn:
Warp yarn: Linen 330gm (11½oz)
Weft yarn: Black = 640gm (22½oz)
   Navy = 510gm (18oz)
   Blue = 430gm (15oz)
   Pale blue = 350gm (12½oz)
Width in reed: 76cm (30in) 150 ends,
   plus extra 4 for the selvedge = 154 ends
Sett: 5 e.p.2.5cm (1in)
Woven length on loom: 1.5m (5ft)
Structure: 2/2 twill on a straight threading: 1, 2, 3, 4
Finishing: Damascus edge and plaited fringe
Weight of finished rug: 1.7kg

Winding the warp: Wind a warp of 154 ends, 3m (10ft) long. Tie the first 6 ends in the first counting tie, then the remainder of the warp in 5s, until the other end, where you will tie 8 in the last counting tie. 30 groups in all.

To wind the warp on the warp beam, follow the instructions on pages 43–47, photos 2.11–2.19. Because this warp is inelastic and needs to be wound on at a tight tension, this is the special method for strong linen warps. Then follow the instructions in photo 2.51, page 67, to tighten each bout. Remember to rock back on your heels so there is a strong pull on each warp bout. It helps if you wind each bout around a short metal bar a couple of times, so you have something to pull on.

Threading: Push across 20 heddles from the right-hand side of the shafts to the centre on each of the four shafts. You will have some spare heddles left in the centre, so just leave the empty heddles in place — they don't interfere with the weaving. Place 2 warp ends in each of the first two heddles, on shafts 1 and 2. This is to strengthen the selvedge. Shafts 3 and 4 have a single warp end in each heddle, so one end is threaded through shaft 3 and one end in shaft 4. Tie these 6 ends in a slip knot. Floor rugs need very firm edges as this is where there is the most wear and tear.

Enter a single warp end in the other heddles until you reach the left-hand selvedge. Thread with a straight draw: 1, 2, 3, 4, check each 8 ends and tie in a slip knot. When you reach the left selvedge, double the ends in the last two shafts. You should have 20 slip knots and end up on shaft 2.

Sleying: The ideal would be to have a 5-dent reed, but these are uncommon. A 10-dent reed can be used, with 1 end in each alternate dent. The outside alternate two dents on each selvedge will have the doubled ends in these dents. For other reeds, see the table in Appendix A, page 175.

Tying on: Make sure the tension is very tight when you tie the warp onto the front rod. Use the surgeon's knot, but when you have checked for mistakes in the threading and checked the tension is even, tie a bow on top of this knot. You will need to place a stick or slat across these bows on the cloth beam when you have woven enough for the weaving to cover them, otherwise there will be bumps which will affect the tension.

Weaving: I prefer ski shuttles (page 73) for weaving rugs because I can load more of the thick yarn onto them. Rug shuttles (page 73) are also satisfactory but they don't glide through the shed as easily as the ski shuttle. Make sure the tension on the warp is very tight.

Weave a heading in plain weave with a single weft yarn to space out the ends on the front rod. Now wind the yarn onto the shuttle, starting with 3 strands at once, to see if this is the correct thickness. The twill weave will cover the warp more easily than a plain weave as it goes over 2 ends at a time. Do a practice few centimetres (inches) in 2/2 twill (figure 3.D, page 82) to check the weft is covering the warp. There is a special way of doing this.

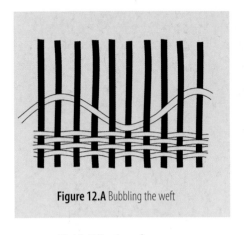

Figure 12.A Bubbling the weft

12.4 Bubbling the weft

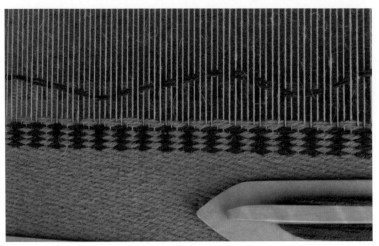

Bubbling the weft: Take the weft pick from one side to the other, leaving it angled upwards when it emerges from the shed at the other side. Starting at the fixed side, push the weft down in a few places so it waves up and down. Change sheds, then beat. This is called beating with a 'closed shed', and the act of closing the shed after changing evens out the bubbles.

Beat with a firm beat; a couple of sharp beats are better than one. You will find that each beat puts pressure on not only the last weft pick, but the ones behind it, so it takes two or 3 weft picks for the weft to cover the warp completely.

If the warp is not completely covered:
- Take away one strand of the weft yarn.
- Tighten the warp.
- Check that you are allowing enough 'bubbles' in the weft.
- If you are using a rising shed loom, you may need to use a rug beater every 5–6cm (3–4in) to add further pressure (photo 12.3, page 155).

Weave for about 10–15cm (4–6in) to make sure you have the beat and coverage right, then leave a 15cm (6in) gap for the beginning fringe. Place enough sticks in the warp to fill in this gap, as this will give you a firm edge to beat against. Now you are ready to begin weaving the rug.

Rug heading: Use the same yarn used as the warp and weave for 1cm (½in) in plain weave, lifting 1 & 3, 2 & 4, alternately. Make sure you bubble the weft sufficiently to cover the warp with no pull-in at the selvedges. The heading should be the exactly the same width as the rug itself as, if it is pulled in at all, the rug will curl at the ends, making an edge that is easy to trip over.

Weaving the rug: Fill the shuttle with two strands of the black weft yarn and weave with a 2/2 twill structure (figure 3.DF, page 82) for 18cm (7in). Because the weft travels over and under 2 warp ends at a time, it is easier to make a firm rug in twill as the weft packs down easily. Remember to bubble the weft.

Black	18cm (7in) black
Black and Navy	2.5cm (1in) black and navy changeover*
Navy	18cm (7in) navy
Navy and Blue	2.5cm (1in) navy and blue changeover*
Blue	18cm (7in) blue
Blue and Pale Blue	2.5cm (1in) blue and pale blue changeover*
Pale Blue	30cm (12in) pale blue
Pale Blue and Blue	2.5cm (1in) pale blue and blue changeover*
Blue	18cm (7in) blue
Blue and Navy	2.5cm (1in) blue and navy changeover*
Navy	18cm (7in) navy
Navy and Black	2.5cm (1in) navy and black changeover*
Black	18cm (7in) black

Figure 12.B Rug design

The colour sequence is:
18cm (7in) black
2.5cm (1in) black and navy changeover*
18cm (7in) navy
2.5cm (1in) navy and blue changeover*
18cm (7in) blue
2.5cm (1in) blue and pale blue changeover*
30cm (12in) pale blue
2.5cm (1in) pale blue and blue changeover*
18cm (7in) blue
2.5cm (1in) blue and navy changeover*
18cm (7in) navy
2.5cm (1in) navy and black changeover*
18cm (7in) black

12.5 Placing the shuttles for tidy selvedges

*For the change in colours, weave the first 2 picks in 1 & 2, 2 & 3 in the new colour, then change to the old colour and weave the next 2 picks in 3 & 4, 4 & 1. This is the twill sequence you have been using, just the colours have changed. Repeat this sequence until you have woven 2.5cm (1in). In this rug five repeats of the sequence were needed for each changeover.

Make sure the twill sequence is the same throughout the entire rug, including the colour change sections. Weave each *changeover sequence for 2.5cm (1in) as stated above.

When changing colours with this thicker weft yarn, tucking in the doubled weft at the edge may let the warp yarn show through. If this happens, split the two weft threads as they leave the selvedge, break off one shorter than the other, and tuck both ends back into the next shed. The new weft ends should also be split into slightly different lengths and overlapped with the old weft. This prevents a doubling of these thick weft yarns. Remember that a join always shows less if the yarn is pulled apart rather than cut.

I have chosen this monochromatic colour sequence as it is easy for you to choose another main colour, other than the blue I have chosen, and to replicate the colour graduations. I have written out the sequence in words so you can cross out the bands of colour as you weave and hopefully you won't lose your way.

The method I have used is an interesting way of changing from one colour to the next without an abrupt change. When you get to these areas of two colours, make sure you place the shuttles in order, i.e. always place the shuttle that has just gone through the shed on the weaving in front of you *behind* the other shuttle. This should give you good selvedges. At the beginning and end of the changeover, you will need to go around the end selvedge thread to cover these threads completely.

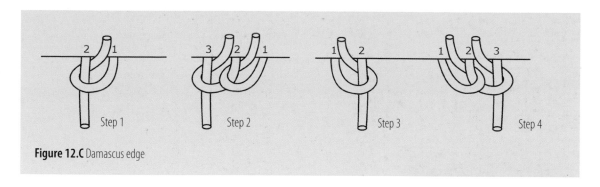

Figure 12.C Damascus edge

Weave the entire length of the rug, remembering to keep the tension tight every time you move the weaving forward. When you reach the end, repeat the heading in the warp yarn, checking to make sure you are not pulling in the edges. Wind the warp on, then cut through the warp, leaving a good 15cm (6in) at the end for the fringe. Unwind the rug off the loom, and cut it off the front rod, also leaving a 15cm (6in) fringe length.

Finishing: This needs to be done as soon as the rug is taken from the loom, as the weaving will come undone very quickly. As floor rugs are subjected to hard wear on all four edges, they need to be firm. The doubled selvedge ends make the sides firm, now you need to strengthen the ends. The best rug finish I have used is described in Peter Collingwood's book mentioned earlier. It is called the Damascus edge.

Knot end 1 around end 2, holding end 2 tight and straight. When you have done this from the right to the left (steps 1 and 2), all the warp ends will be lying back up over the rug. Turn the rug over, start from the left edge and repeat the knot (steps 3 and 4) and all the ends will then be lying out from the edge.

The last stage is to plait these ends in a three-end plait or twist the ends as on page 151. Tie the ends in an overhand knot (page 86) and trim tidily, leaving about a 5–7cm (2–3in) plait.

Check both sides of the rug for any loose ends and trim these. Floor rugs do not need washing or pressing.

Although this is a big project, it is well worthwhile and you will have many years of walking on and admiring your rug.

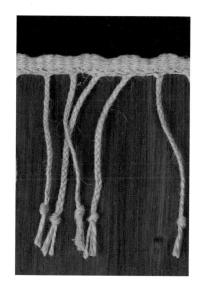

12.6 Damascus edge

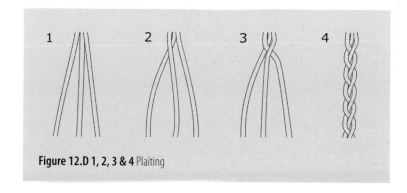

Figure 12.D 1, 2, 3 & 4 Plaiting

Ask yourself:

- Did I enjoy this project?
- What parts did I enjoy the most?
- What parts did I not enjoy doing?
- What did I learn?
- What can I improve about the finished project?

161

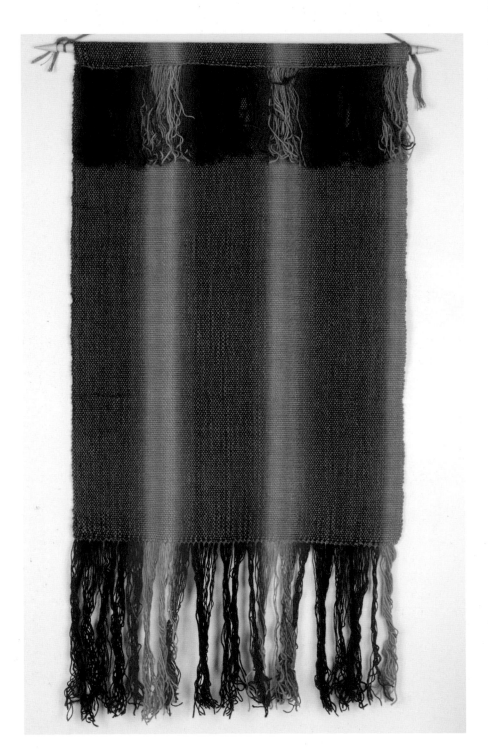

13.1 Hanging

You will learn how to weave with space-dyed warps

Minimum loom width: 46cm (18in)

Wall hangings are fun to weave because there are no boundaries. They don't have to be washable, soft, hard-wearing, flexible or a certain shape. The only characteristic is that they should be decorative.

I love multi-coloured warps and I often dye my own. But there are so many beautiful dyed yarns on the market now that we have a plethora to choose from. When I dye my own warps, I use a random dye method. That sounds grand but it really means I put colour on wherever I feel like it. Commercial yarn manufacturers don't have that luxury. Their yarn is space dyed, and there are repeats to the colour sequence. The advantage of this is that the repeats form a pattern.

So we will take advantage of that space dyeing for a wall hanging. Some of the most beautiful space-dyed yarns are made for knitting socks. I have a lot of friends who knit socks and I have often admired the choice of beautiful yarns available to them. Sock yarns also have the added advantage that they are usually reinforced for harder wear.

I had great fun on the internet choosing the yarn for this wall hanging. This space-dyed yarn is from Germany. It is called Zauberball. It is made by Schoppel Wolle and is readily available from many stockists (Appendix B, page 178). It is 25% nylon, 75% wool. It is easy to work out how much yarn there is as the length is on the label, 420m (455yd) for a 100gm (3½oz) ball.

With the added nylon the wool is strong enough for a warp, even though it is a single strand yarn. Usually yarn needs to be plied to make it strong enough for a warp. To test for warp strength, stretch a length of the yarn over your thumbnail and tug. If it breaks easily it is not suitable for a warp, but can be used as a weft.

There are many other space-dyed wools that would give the same effect and the other fun part of this type of yarn and weaving is that you never quite know what the colours in the hanging will look like until you wind the warp. The bright yarn I chose looked like photo 13.4, page 164, when I put the warp on the loom, so I know it was going to be fun to weave.

Because all the colour emphasis is on the warp, I have chosen to

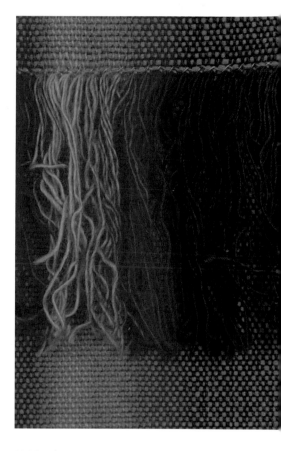

13.2 Detail

13.3 Yarn used

163

13.4 Warp on loom through the raddle

make the warp the dominant feature. So it is sett close together for a warp-dominant weave. This is a good weave structure for a wall hanging as the heavy warp will give weight lengthwise.

A warp-faced weave is one where the warp is closely sett so the weft does not show at all. As the warp yarn was wool, I did not make this a completely warp-faced cloth, as the wool warp ends would have been so close that the ends would have stuck together and made it difficult to get a clear shed.

If you want a wider hanging with two balls of yarn, remember the space dyeing is measured out by the manufacturer. Make sure the join between the two balls carries on the colour sequence. Lay the end of one ball over the beginning of the next ball, and move the yarns up and down until the colour sequence continues in the same order.

If there is a knot in the yarn (there shouldn't be with this space-dyed yarn), again make sure the colour sequence is correct.

To allow for the warp to show up, the weft should be about three times thicker than the warp. I tried various colours and thicknesses of weft yarn at the beginning of the hanging to see which I preferred. I chose the orange because I wanted to emphasise the yellow/orange warp colours. Having a large stash of yarn helps; I have a wide range of yarns and colours to choose from.

WARP PLAN

Warp yarn: Zauberball — Fushseinbeet is the colour I have chosen, and this comes as 420m (459yd) per 100gm (3½oz) ball.

Wraps: 22 per 2.5cm (1in)

Weft yarn: Orange wool, Tex 110/3 9672m/kg (4800yd/lb)

Wraps: Single strand 30 per 2.5cm (1in). I used 6 strands wound on the shuttle together.

Warp length: Hanging = 60cm (23½in)
Wastage = 91cm (36in)
Total warp = 1.5m (5ft)

Weight of warp and weft required: Warp = 100gm (3½oz)
Weft = 75gm (2½oz)

Warp width. I wound the warp until I ran out of yarn. I actually got a warp 46cm (18in) wide, so the length of yarn on the label was on the generous side.

Width in reed: 46cm (18in) 288 ends

Sett: 16 e.p.2.5cm (1in)

Reed: 8-dent

Woven length on loom: 60cm (23½in)

Threading: Straight draw 1, 2, 3, 4

Structure: Warp-dominant

Finishing: Hemstitching

Weight of finished hanging: 170gm (6oz)

Winding the warp: Wind a warp 1.5m (5ft) long until the ball is finished. Keep any leftover pieces of yarn in case you have a broken thread. Although this is a very short warp, wind with two crosses as the sett is close and the wool will stick together otherwise. Tie a counting tie around every 16 ends. There should be 18 ties.

Take extra care that the warp ends don't break during the warping or any of the following processes. Because of the space-dyed colour sequence, it is not easy to mend a broken end with the matching colour. If a thread does break, put in a replacement end in any colour, and when the weaving is off the loom, you can use some of the waste yarn to darn in a matching thread.

Threading: Push across 36 heddles from the right-hand side and thread 1, 2, 3, 4. Check and tie every 16 ends to give you 18 slip knots.

Sleying: Use an 8-dent reed and place 2 ends in each dent. For other reed sizes, see Appendix A, page 175.

Tying on: Tie on with as little wastage as possible. This knotted end will also be the fringe so it is not really wasted.

Weaving: Weave a heading, then place a stick across to leave room to hemstitch. Wind 6 strands of the fine weft yarn together on the shuttle. I tried various weft sizes and colours at the beginning of the warp to see which I liked best. Black was my first choice but it darkened the warp colours. The orange seemed the best for this warp. I undid this sampling when I had chosen the right colour because I didn't want to waste any of this precious warp.

Weave in plain weave (1 & 3, 2 & 4), beating firmly, for a few centimetres (inches), then hemstitch in fours. The thick weft shows as it curves around the selvedge ends so watch the selvedges as you weave. It is very quick weaving as the weft is so thick.

Weave for 60cm (23½in) or until you run out of warp. Some looms need more waste yarn than others. I was able to weave for 76cm (30in) before I had to stop. Hemstitch the end and cut the hanging from the loom, leaving 13cm (5in) of fringe at this end. Remove the heading from the beginning of the warp.

Finishing: There is no need to wash the hanging, but a press with a damp cloth will help the finished appearance.

Turn the fabric under and sew a hem at the top end, big enough for the rod to go through. I chose a rod with finials at each end. At the lower end of the hanging, leave the fringe loose as the yarn colours are so attractive. As the hanging does not move much or need washing, the fringe can be left untwisted.

Because the warp colours are so brilliant, I left the warp fringe hanging down from the top.

13.5 Weaving on loom

Ask yourself:
- Did I enjoy this project?
- What parts did I enjoy the most?
- What parts did I not enjoy doing?
- What did I learn?
- What can I improve about the finished project?

14.1 Wrap-around

Wrap-around

You will learn how to weave fabric for clothing

Minimum loom width: 76cm (30in)
Number of heddles required: 720
4 or 8-shaft loom

It is very satisfying to wear clothing that you have woven and made yourself, but it took many years of weaving before I could get up enough courage to cut into my woven fabric. I was sure it would fall to pieces before my eyes once I took the scissors to it. Thinking back to my first attempts, I was right. In the beginning I wove with thick yarns because they were quicker to warp and thread. I was so slow at everything that the thought of weaving fabric with over 16 ends to 2.5cm (1in) was too much.

However, as I became quicker, the finer yarns became less daunting. In the beginning I wove cloth for garments that didn't need cutting, like the cocoon in Chapter 8. But as I gained confidence I began to weave finer, more stable cloth that could be cut. I also learnt about finishing the cloth to make it firm enough to hold together.

Clothing fabric should be:

- stable
- flexible
- unique

CHARACTERISTICS

Stable: Wool and cotton are yarns that will mesh together with washing to form a stable fabric. I have woven silk fabric but at a sett of 60 ends per 2.5cm (1in), I would not recommend fine silk for a beginner. Patterns with long floats are not suitable as these weaken the fabric and can pull. For this garment I have chosen to work with wool; I find this is the easiest yarn to use as it can be finished to make a very stable cloth.

Flexible: The fabric needs to be firm but not stiff because you need movement as the clothing fits around your body. Therefore fine threads are best, as these can be sett closely without losing flexibility.

Unique: Apart from the satisfaction of wearing cloth you have woven, I can't see the point of weaving fabric that industrial machines can do faster and cheaper. For example, I will not weave a denim cloth for jeans, but I will weave fabric to my original design and colours, ensuring there will never be another garment like mine. As

14.2 Woven wrap-around pinned to one side

a production weaver I found that buyers valued this uniqueness and were willing to pay for those attributes. And as a teacher, I found that wearing my own garments showed my students what they could do.

A good width for most garments is 76cm (30in). With fulling, this will reduce to 69cm (27in), which is what was called a 'tailor's width'. This width means there is no need for a centre back seam. However, if the finished cloth for this wrap-around measures 76cm (30in) wide when finished, the garment is more versatile. Remember there is always draw-in at the selvedges as well as shrinkage to take into account. Therefore a loom width of 82cm (32in) will give you more scope. Because I lost my big loom in the Christchurch earthquakes, my largest loom now measures 76cm (30in), so I have added these measurements (in italics) as well. The wrap-around in photos 14.1 (page 166), 14.2 (page 167) and 14.4 (page 173) was made on this loom. If you do have an 82cm (32in) wide loom, just add a further 2.5cm (1in) each side in the black yarn. I have added the measurements for the larger 82cm (32in) width loom in italics (the calico mock-up garment in photos 14.3a, b and c, page 172). This size does give you a more versatile garment.

The garment I have planned is simple, can be worn several ways and requires the minimum of cutting. I have chosen the dramatic colourway of black, grey and white, grading the colours into one another so there is no sudden transition of one to the next. This three-colour cloth can be woven with any other colours. Navy, blue and pale blue would be one example, and would give the same dramatic appearance.

For the weft yarn I usually choose the intermediate colour, in this case the grey, but I had a play with the three colours at the beginning of the warp to see which combination I liked the best.

WARP PLAN

Because there are 720 warp ends (*768*), check that you have enough heddles before you start. Although this is a four-shaft draft, sometimes I use the eight shafts on my Baby Wolf loom as I need those extra heddles. Spreading out the threads over more shafts also reduces the friction of closely sett yarns.

Warp yarn: Black, white and grey fine wools 110/3 merino wool, 9672m/kg (4800yd/lb)

Wraps: 32 per 2.5cm (1in)

Warp length: Wrap-around, including fringes = 178cm (70in)
Wastage = 91cm (36in)
Total warp (rounded up) = 3m (10ft)
I have added a extra few centimetres (inches) to allow some practice at the beginning.

Weft yarn: Grey, same as the warp

Weight of warp and weft required: Black = 150gm (5¼oz)
Grey = 250gm (9oz)
White = 150gm (5¼oz)

Width in reed: 76cm (30in) 720 ends. (*82cm (32in) 768 ends*)

Sett: 24 e.p.2.5cm (1in)
24 p.p.2.5cm (1in)
Reed: 8 or 12-dent
Woven length on loom: 168cm (66in)
Threading: Straight draw
Structure: 2/2 twill
Finished size after washing: Length 155cm (61in), width 67cm
(26½in)*. *Length 160cm (63in), width 76cm (30in)*
*Because I used a fine merino wool, I found the shrinkage was high,
especially in the width. With different wool, there would be less
shrinkage. However, because this is such a versatile garment, the
finished size is not crucial.
Finishing: Hemstitching
Weight of finished fabric: 200gm (7oz)
Winding the warp: For a 76cm (30in) loom width, wind a warp 3m
(10ft) long and 76cm (30in) wide as this will give you some spare warp
to try out different colour combinations. Wind the warp in four sections
as this prevents build-up on your warping board or mill. Make a cross
at each end as the wool will be somewhat sticky. When winding the
two-colour sections, wind them together as described on page 62, with
two ends under the cross and two ends over, as this will make it quicker.
Place the counting tie around every 24 ends to give you 30 ties in all.

If your loom width is 81cm (32in) wide, add an extra 2.5cm (1in) each
side in the black — 32 ties.

Warp colours: Wind 13cm (5in) black
2.5cm (1in) grey and black
13cm (5in) grey
2.5cm (1in) grey and white
15cm (6in) white
2.5cm (1in) grey and white
13cm (5in) grey
2.5cm (1in) grey and black
13cm (5in) black

When I chose the yarns from my stash, I only had two smaller cones
of grey wool reasonably close in colour, so I wound these together,
separating the two strands with my fingers. This makes for an interesting
blend of the greys. When I threaded the grey section, I had to make sure
that the lighter grey was on shafts 1 & 3, and the darker grey on shafts
2 & 4. This is a good trick to know if you have two colours which are
the same but have different batch numbers. I can remember weaving
at night, finishing one cone and beginning another cone of the same
colour without noticing the two different batch numbers. In the
morning, in better light, the change was quite noticeable.
Threading: For a 76cm (30in) width on a 4-shaft loom, you will need
180 heddles on each shaft. Push across 90 heddles on each shaft from
the right to the centre. Thread with a straight draw: 1, 2, 3, 4. Put a slip
knot around every 24 ends to give you 30 slip knots.

For an 82cm (32in) wide loom, you will need 192 heddles on each shaft. Push across 96 heddles on each shaft to the centre. You will end up with 32 slip knots.

Sleying: With an 8-dent reed, place 3 ends in each space. With a 12-dent reed, place 2 ends in each space. For other reed sizes, see Appendix A, page 175.

Weaving: Weave a heading, then weave in 2/2 twill (figures 3.DT and 3.DF, page 82) for about 2.5cm (1in) in each of the three warp colours to see which combination you like best. You can see in photo 14.1, page 166, that I chose the grey for the weft.

Leave a small gap, and begin weaving the fabric, hemstitching after you have woven about 2.5cm (1in). Remember to coordinate the shuttle and hand (table looms) or feet (floor looms) movements as this will ensure a good rhythm and prevent mistakes. When the shuttle is beginning from the right, use your right hand or foot to change the shed, and vice versa. I also find saying the twill sequence to myself helps.

Beat with 24 picks to 2.5cm (1in). This needs to be a balanced cloth with an equal number of warp and weft threads showing. The angle of the twill should be 45 degrees. You may need to measure the first few centimetres (inches) to check.

Weave for 168cm (66in). This allows for the draw-in and shrinkage that will happen when the cloth is taken off the loom and fulled. Because this garment is so versatile, it does not matter if your shrinkage and draw-in rate is slightly different. Hemstitch the end and cut the fabric off, leaving about 7cm (3in) for a fringe or the hem at both ends.

Finishing: To make sure the fabric doesn't fall to bits when it is cut, the finishing needs to be vigorous. Fulling is almost like felting the cloth very slightly, so all the threads mesh together. I use the bath for this. Place enough hot soapy water in the bath so the water will completely cover the fabric. The water should be hand hot. Place the fabric in the bath in folds, and refold it several times, moving the cloth through the water. You don't actually want the cloth to felt, so check all the time.

Pull out the plug and let the water drain out, leaving the fabric in the bath, then re-fill the bath with warm water (no soap) and rinse. Make sure the tap doesn't run onto the fabric. Pull out the plug again and leave the fabric in the bath for about an hour to let most of the water drain off. I don't put the fabric in the washing machine for a final spin, as this can leave creases in the cloth.

To dry, lay the cloth flat on several towels over a piece of plastic sheeting on a table or bed. It may take a day or two to dry, depending on the temperature. If you lay the fabric over a clothes line or drying rack you get marks which are hard to get rid of. Do not tumble dry.

When I wove many long lengths of fabric, I used a slatted roller and rolled the cloth around the roller, smoothing it flat with my hands as I rolled. Then every day I re-wound the cloth so the inside had a chance to dry.

Press while slightly damp with your iron on a wool setting. Don't slide

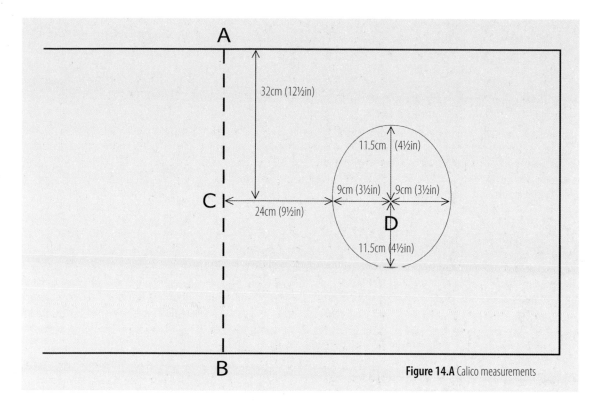

Figure 14.A Calico measurements

the iron over the cloth; it is an up-and-down motion rather than a side-to-side one. You can tell when the fabric is stable because if you run your thumbnail firmly over the fabric, the yarns should not move at all.

To make up: It is easier and less scary to make a mock-up piece first before you cut into the finished woven fabric. Cut out a piece of calico or old sheeting the exact size of your finished fabric. Fold the calico in half lengthwise (fringe to fringe) and mark this point at both selvedges (felt pens are good for marking). Draw a dotted line on the calico between these two selvedge marks (A–B). I have used the measurements for my woven wrap-around, but you can adjust this later to fit you.

Now measure 32cm (12½in) down from one of the selvedge markers along the dotted line and mark this point. Measure another 32cm (12½in) in from this point down the calico length (C–D). This mark will be the centre of the armhole. From this point, D, make four lines radiating out to outline the armhole as in figure 14.A. The lengthwise measurement is 9cm (3½in) each side of point D. The widthwise measurement is 11.5cm (4½in) each side of point D. Join these marks to make the armhole. Repeat for the other armhole.

Cut the armholes out of the calico and try the garment on. As the wrap-around will be worn over a top of some type, make sure there is some slack (photos 14.3a, b and c, page 172). Now adjust the armholes to fit. Again draw on the calico where the armholes should be. You may need an assistant for this.

171

14.3a Front, calico mock-up with the armhole worn near the top edge

14.3b Back, calico mock-up with the armhole worn near the top edge

14.3c Front, calico mock-up with armhole worn near the lower edge

Because I only had a 76cm (30in) loom and my fabric shrank more than I expected, my armholes are about in the centre of the garment, as in photos 14.1, 14.2 and 14.4. If you have a wider fabric width, the armholes will be off centre and you will have a more versatile garment (see photos above). However, the measurements given above work for both sizes.

When you are satisfied that your calico mock-up is the right size, pin it onto your woven finished fabric and mark the armholes with tailor's chalk or tacking thread. If you are really worried that the fabric will fall to bits, run a zigzag stitch (not an overlocking stitch) around the chalk or tacking marks.

Now comes the bold step. Take a deep breath and bravely take up your scissors. Cut out the armholes. There is no right or wrong side to this fabric. With a matching bias tape machine sew the tape to the outside edges of the armholes. Turn the fabric inside out and hand sew the tape to the inside edge. As bias tape is stretchy, it will fit around the curves.

Now you have some choices. If your selvedges are neat enough, leave them as the top and lower ends of the garment. If they are untidy, just turn them under once and hand sew to the inside, or add the bias tape to neaten the edges.

The raw ends can be left as a fringe as you have neatly hemstitched both ends. If you don't want a fringe, trim it off close to the hemstitching and turn under for a hem.

Wearing the garment: If your fabric width is 82cm (32in) when finished, as in the calico mock-up photos above, the armholes are not placed in the centre and you can wear this wrap-around many different ways as shown. There are probably even more ways than this!

Ask yourself:

- Did I enjoy this project?
- What parts did I enjoy the most?
- What parts did I not enjoy doing?
- What did I learn?
- What can I improve about the finished project?

14.4 Woven wrap-around worn with the two fronts pinned together

Appendix A

REED TABLE

	Dents per 2.5cm (1in)							
Order of sley	**5**	**6**	**8**	**10**	**12**	**14**	**15**	**16**
0~0~1	2	2	3	3	4	5	5	5
0~1	2½	3	4	5	6	7	7½	8
0~1~1	3	4	5	7	8	9	10	11
0~1~1~1	4	4½	6	7½	9	10½	11½	12
1	5	6	8	10	12	14	15	16
1~1~1~2	6	7½	10	12½	15	17½	19	20
1~1~2	7	8	11	13	16	19	20	21
1~2	7½	9	12	15	18	21	22½	24
1~2~2	8	10	13	17	20	23	25	27
1~2~2~2	9	10½	14	17½	21	24½	26	28
2	10	12	16	20	24	28	30	32
2~2~2~3	11	13½	18	22½	27	31½	34	36
2~3	12½	15	20	25	30	33	37½	40
2~3~3	13	16	21	27	32	35	40	43
2~3~3~3	14	16½	22	27½	33	37	41	44
3	15	18	24	30	36	38½	45	48
3~3~3~4	16	19½	26	32½	39	42	49	52

Ends per 2.5cm (1in)

Appendix B

YARNS

I have tried to use readily available yarns in all these projects. I have listed the yarn sources I used but there are many other sources of these yarns. Google is a good way to find suppliers close to you. The full website addresses are listed at the end of this appendix. Where I have used yarns from my considerable stash, I have given the suppliers of similar yarns.

Chapter 2: Warping the Loom and Chapter 3: Weaving
Warp and weft yarn: Medium weight wool. 2015m/kg (1000yd/lb).
Wraps: 16 per 2.5cm (1in).
Supplier: The yarn used in this project is very similar to a wool yarn from Webs.

Chapter 4: Table Runners
Warp and weft yarn: Warp and weft. Cottolin 22/2 Bockens Nialin. 6590m/kg (3270yd/lb).
Wraps: 34 per 2.5cm (1in).
Supplier: Glenora Weaving.

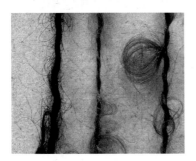

Chapter 5: Mohair Wrap
Warp and weft yarn: Warp and weft. Mohair 2015m/kg (1000yd/lb).
Wraps: 12 per 2.5cm (1in).
Supplier: The yarn used in this project is very similar to mohair loop yarn from Webs: 78% mohair, 13% wool, 9% nylon.

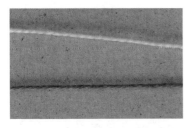

Chapter 6: Dish Towels
Warp and weft yarn: White and pink 8/2 mercerised cotton 6770m/kg (3360yd/lb).
Wraps: 32 per 2.5cm (1in).
Supplier: This cotton yarn is available from most weaving yarn sources.

Chapter 7: Table Mats
Warp and weft yarn: 5/2 yellow mercerised cotton. 4231m/kg (2100yd/lb).
Wraps: 32 ends per 2.5cm (1in).
Supplier: This cotton yarn is available from most weaving yarn sources.

Chapter 8: Reversible Cocoon Jacket
Warp yarn: Black, 110/3 wool 9672m/kg (4800yd/lb).
Wraps: 30 per 2.5cm (1in).
Supplier: This yarn is readily available from many weaving or machine knitting suppliers.
Weft yarn: Upper layer – purple brushed mohair. 1995/kg (990yd/lb).
Wraps: 10 wraps per 2.5cm (1in).
Weft: Lower layer – black looped mohair. 2015m/kg (1000yd/lb).
Wraps: 12 wraps per 2.5cm (1in). This is the same yarn used in Chapter 5.

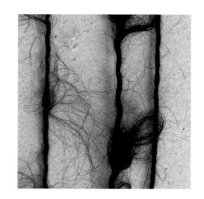

Chapter 9: Cushion Covers
Warp and weft yarn: Background white wool 2539m/kg (1260yd/lb) Tex 180/3.
Wraps: 20 per 2.5cm (1in).
Pattern green wool 2015m/kg (1000yd/lb).
Wraps: 16 per 2.5cm (1in).
Supplier: These wool yarns are available from many yarn suppliers.

Chapter 10: Scarf
Warp and weft yarn: Background: Variegated tencel 8/2 6770m/kg (3360yd/lb).
Wraps: 40 wraps per 2.5cm (1in).
Suppliers: Webs.
Wandering warp yarn: Variegated rayon ribbon.
Wraps: 3 wraps per 2.5cm (1in).
Supplier: Available from many yarn suppliers or found in bins in knitting shops.

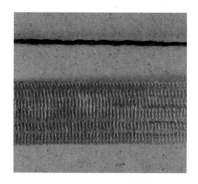

Chapter 11: Ruffle Scarf
Warp yarn: Black colcolastic for centre stripe. Nm 34/2. One mini spool holds 50gm (1¾oz).
Wraps: 48 per 2.5cm (1in).
Supplier: Fibreholics.
Warp and weft yarn: Teal 10/2 bamboo for side stripes, 8463m/kg (4200yd/lb).
Wraps: 40 per 2.5cm (1in).
Supplier: Available from many yarn suppliers.

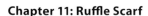

Chapter 12: Weft-faced Floor Rug
Warp yarn: Linen 8/5 881m/kg (437yd/lb). Or linen 8/6 812m/kg (403yd/lb).
Wraps: 12 per 2.5cm (1in).
Suppliers: Linen 8/5, 8/6, Webs and Glenora Weaving.
Linen 10/6 nel (6/6Mn), Handweavers Studio.
Seine twine, Glenora Weaving.
Weft yarn: 2 ply rug wool. In colours ranging from black to pale blue.
Wraps: 11 per 2.5cm (1in). Used two fold.
Suppliers: Rug wool, Collingwood rug yarn, Yarn Barn and Webs.
Rug yarn, Glenora Weaving and Handweavers Studio.

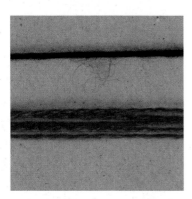

Chapter 13: Spaced-dyed Warp Hanging
Warp yarn: Zauberball (Fushseinbeet is the colour I have chosen) which comes as 420m (459yd) per 100gm (3½oz) ball.
Wraps: 22 per 2.5cm (1in).
Supplier: Vintage Purls.
Weft yarn: Orange wool, Tex 110/3 9672m/kg (4800yd/lb).
Wraps: Single strand 30 per 2.5cm (1in). I used 6 strands wound on the shuttle together.
Supplier: This yarn is readily available from many weaving or machine knitting suppliers.

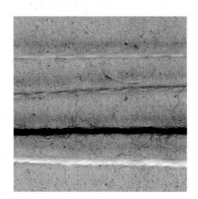

Chapter 14: Wrap-around
Warp and weft yarn: Black, white and grey fine wools 110/3 merino. wool, 9672m/kg (4800yd/lb).
Wraps: 32 per 2.5cm (1in).
Supplier: This yarn is readily available from many weaving or machine knitting suppliers.

SUPPLIERS
Ashford Handicrafts, New Zealand www.ashford.co.nz
Camilla Valley Farm Weavers, Canada camillavalleyfarm.com
Fibreholics, New Zealand www.fibreholics.co.nz
Glenora Weaving, Australia www.glenoraweaving.com.au
Halcyon Yarns, USA www.halcyonyarns.com
Handweavers Studio, UK www.handweavers.co.uk
Jane Stafford Yarns, Canada www.janestaffordtextiles.com
Schoppel Wolle, Germany www.schoppel-wolle.de
Venne Colcoton, Netherlands www.vennecolcoton.com
Vintage Purls, New Zealand www.vintagepurls.co.nz
Webs, USA www.yarn.com
Yarn Barn, USA www.yarnbarn-ks.com

Appendix C

BURN TESTS FOR IDENTIFYING YARNS

If you are having trouble identifying what sort of yarn you have, it can be helpful to do a burn test. Just break a piece of yarn off and place it over a flame and see how it burns, note the smell and what the ash looks like. The table below explains the results from a variety of fibres.

Disclaimer: As with all things related to fire, care and caution is required when doing these tests, which should be undertaken at your own risk. The author and publisher cannot be held responsible in the unlikely event of any mishap occurring.

YARN	HOW IT BURNS	SMELL	ASH
Wool	Burns slowly and self-extinguishes, curls away from the flame.	Hair.	Dark crumbly ash.
Silk	Burns slowly and self-extinguishes.	Hair or eggs.	Black, holds its shape but is crushable.
Linen	Burns quickly and continues to glow when removed from flame.	Burning grass.	Gray feathery ash.
Cotton	Burns quickly in open flame and continues to glow when removed from the flame.	Burning paper.	Gray feathery ash.
Alpaca	Hard to ignite.	Strong smell of burned hair.	Shiny ash that keeps its shape.
Rayon	Burns quickly in open flame. Not self-extinguishing.	Burning leaves or paper.	Black or grey feathery ash.
Acrylic	Ignites immediately. Melts and melted drops continue to burn.	Toxic fumes.	Hard black bead.
Polyester	Burns slowly, and melts in open flame. Self-extinguishing when removed from flame.	Sweetish smell.	Hard black bead.

Appendix D

OTHER WAYS OF WRITING DRAFTS

Unfortunately, there is no standard way of writing weaving drafts, and each writer seems to have their favourite way of doing things. When you see drafts in other books and magazines look for the section that explains how they are written. For example, one of my early weaving books by Marguerite Porter Davison, *A Handweaver's Pattern Book*, was for sinking shed looms, so each shaft marked in the treadling draft meant a shaft was lowered, not lifted. Whenever a weaver said all her weaving was upside down, we all knew she had been following this pattern book.

Order of reading: The four quadrants are common to all drafts, but the order of reading them will differ. Some treadling drafts are written from the bottom up, some have the threading drafts at the bottom of the page and so on. Some weavers prefer this because the draft corresponds to the position of the weft as you weave. On the loom the weaving grows away from you, i.e. from the bottom up.

Numbers: The black squares are replaced by numbers or marks and this is a common way to write drafts. My table loom drafts have numbers instead of black squares.

Symbols: These will have a chart to tell you what the symbols mean. For example, a T might mean a thick thread and an F a fine thread.

Countermarch tie-up: With a countermarch loom each shaft is tied to either a sinking or rising lamm (page 25). Sometimes the tie-up is written with an 0 for a rising shed (think of 0 as a bubble, which rises), and an X for a sinking shaft.

Colour: Colours can be added to the drafts to differentiate the warp and weft threads.

Tromp as writ: This is an old-fashioned term that is still used. It means the threading (writ) is the same as the treadling (tromp). See drafts in Chapter 7, figures 7.AT (page 113) and 7.AF (page 114).

COMPUTERS IN WEAVING

When I first began to weave and figured out how to use pattern drafts in weaving books, I followed the drafts. Eventually I began to write my own, and although what I 'invented' was probably written down in some book, I did learn a lot from the process, using graph paper and coloured pencils.

This is a slow way of writing out drafts, and with the coming of computers the whole process was speeded up considerably. In minutes I could generate drafts that had taken me hours before. Also with computer drafts, you need only write in the threading, tie-up and treadling quadrants and the draw-downs would automatically appear. In the beginning I thought this was magical and would play for hours. Then I graduated to a computer-assisted loom page 33) where the treadling sequence went from the computer directly to the loom.

The limit with any floor loom (apart from dobby and computer-assisted looms), is the number of treadles. If your loom has six treadles then you can only have six combinations of shaft to treadle tie-ups in one piece of cloth without changing the treadle tie-ups. This is where table looms come into their own, as any shaft combination is possible at any time.

With ten treadles you can have ten combinations. More than ten treadles is too wide for our feet to comfortably reach. With a 4-shaft loom, there are 14 possible combinations, listed below:

1 & 3
2 & 4
1 & 2
2 & 3
3 & 4
4 & 1
1, 2, 3
2, 3, 4
3, 4, 1
4, 1, 2
1
2
3
4

On a table loom each shaft is lifted individually so theoretically on a four-shaft table loom, you could use all 14 combinations in one piece of cloth. The result might look a bit busy but it is possible.

With an 8-shaft loom the number of combinations is increased, with 16 shafts there are thousands of combinations. Now that multi-shaft weaving is becoming more popular, computer-assisted weaving is being used more. Not only can I use any number of combinations in one cloth, I don't have to crawl underneath my loom to change the tie-ups.

If you are at ease with using a computer and once you have done some weaving and are becoming familiar with weaving drafts, try some of the weaving software. Many of them can be downloaded for a month's free trial.

www.avlusa.com
www.pixeLoom.com
www.fiberworks-pcw.com
www.weaveit.com
www.weavemaker.com

Glossary

Balanced weave: A weave where the yarn size and number of threads per inch are the same for both warp and weft.

Beaming: Winding the warp onto the loom.

Beater: Frame, holding the reed, which beats the weft into position.

Binder: Plain weft threads which hold or bind the pattern weft.

Bobbin: The cylinder on which yarn or thread is wound.

Bout: A group of warp ends.

Castle: Frame on loom from which the shafts are suspended.

Count: The size of the yarn.

Creel: A frame for holding bobbins in the correct position while winding.

Cross: Crossing the threads during warping ensures they stay in their correct order.

Cross stick: Stick inserted in the cross during beaming and warping.

Dent: Space in reed.

Draft: Diagram of threading and weaving order.

Draw-down: Diagram on graph paper of the finished, woven cloth.

Draw-in: Amount weaving will narrow while being woven.

End: A warp thread.

Fell: The edge of the weaving at the last weft pick.

Float: A thread passing over two or more warp or weft threads.

Fulling: Finishing process for woollen fabrics.

Hank: A specific length of yarn or thread based on the type of fibre.

Heading: The first rows in a new warp.

Heddle: Needle-like wire or string holders of the warp threads.

Intersection: Position at which the warp crosses over or under the weft.

Jack: A pivoted wooden or metal bar.

Lamm: A horizontal bar on some looms that connects the shaft to the treadles.

Pick: A single weft row.

Pirn: The spool of a shuttle.

Raddle: Spaces the warp as it is wound onto the loom.

Reed: Metal, comb-like piece, set in the beater to separate and beat the threads.

Selvedge: Outside warp threads that strengthen the fabric edges.

Sett: Number of warp threads per centimetre (inch) threaded in the reed.

Shaft: Frame that holds the heddles.

Shed: Opening formed in the warp, through which the shuttle passes.

Shuttle: The yarn holder.

Sley: To thread warp ends through the reed.

Slub: A type of yarn with irregularities that give texture to the cloth.

Tabby: Plain weave structure.

Tex: Metric method of measuring the length of yarn.

Tie-up: The act of connecting the correct shafts to each treadle.

Treadle: The foot-operated pedal on a loom.

Twill: Structure where the weft threads are woven in a diagonal pattern.

Warp: Lengthwise threads on loom.

Warping frame or mill: Frame, with movable pegs, onto which warp ends are strung prior to putting the threads on the loom.

Weft: Widthwise threads on the loom.

Bibliography

Collapse Weave, Creating Three Dimensional Cloth, Anne Field; David Bateman Ltd, NZ, 2010; Trafalgar Square Books, USA, 2008 & Bloomsbury, UK, 2008

Contemporary Weaving Patterns, Margo Selby; A&C Black, UK, 2012

Color and Fiber, Patricia Lambert, Barbara Staepelaere, Mary G. Fry; Schiffer Publishing Co., USA, 1986

The Key to Weaving, Mary E Black; 2nd Rev. ed.; Macmillan, USA, 1980

Dévoré for Weavers and Knitters, Anne Field; Trafalgar Square Books, USA, 2010

Double Weave on Four to Eight Shafts, Ursina Arn-Grischott; Interweave Press, USA, 1999

Mastering Weave Structures, Sharon Alderman; Interweave Press, USA, 2004

Magic in the Water, Wet Finishing Handwovens, Laura Fry; Fry Weaving Studio, Canada, 2002

New Guide to Weaving, Peggy Osterkamp; Book I, 2, 3; Lease Sticks Press, USA, (book 3) 2007

The Ashford Book of Weaving for the Four Shaft Loom, Anne Field; Ashford Handicrafts, NZ, 2007

The Complete Book of Drafting for Handweavers, Madelyn Van der Hoogt; Shuttlecraft Books, USA,1993

The Techniques of Rug Weaving, Peter Collingwood; Watson-Guptill, USA, 1968

Weaver's Companion, Handwoven Magazine; Interweave Press, USA, 2001

■ MAGAZINES FOR WEAVERS

Handwoven, USA

Shuttle, Spindle and Dyepot, USA

Fiberarts, USA

Creative Fibre, NZ

Vavmagasinet, Scandinavia

Weavers Craft, USA

The Journal for Weavers, Spinners and Dyers, UK

Textile Fibre Forum, Australia

Index